At this pivotal moment in human...... ... this anthology are more essential than ever before, in bringing understanding, healing, and transformation to our world. The powerful insights, wisdom, and revelations in this volume are only derived from personal, lived experience and only conveyed through the power of poetry. Social justice is not only the theme of these empowering verses; it is also served, and the Beloved Community advanced, through these Rising Voices.

Dan Hocoy, PhD
President, Goddard College
Co-Editor, *Shadows & Light: Theory, Research, and Practice in Transpersonal Psychology* (Vols. 1 & 2)

The poems in *Rising Voices*, like powerful anthems, call for a relationally ethical connection between heart and mind by evoking emotions, prompting meaningful questions, critical reflections, and generating insights into uniquely lived local experiences otherwise foreclosed by intellectualism, lost in generalized narratives, and ignored by disaffection.

Héctor Luis Vargas, PhD
Full Professor, Regis University

It is with distinct pleasure that I endorse *Rising Voices*, a compelling portrayal of life identifying everyday issues that are real and present. I found that each poem is distinctive and personal to the poet, yet the longings and sufferings are shared by us all. The authors do our country a great service toward understanding the multiculturalism and diversity that exists in the United States. My hats off and a salute to all the great poets who contributed to this book.

Michael Colombe
Candidate for U.S House of Representatives, Colorado 5th Congressional District

This is not just a book of poems, but also expressions of black history through poetic self-reflections. When you read this book, you will be able to free your mind and enlightenment will follow.

Dr. Regina A. Lewis
CEO of ReginaSpeaking, LLC

As always with the Poetry, Healing, and Growth Series books, I find myself enthralled, breathless, and sobbing as I read the poems in *Rising Voices*. The pain, the triumph, and the joy seep through the pages and into my soul. Reading these poems is an opportunity to bear witness to the experience of what it is like to live in the skin of someone who has felt the pain of being unseen, rejected, unwanted, kicked out, shamed, and despondent. I believe that "love means never looking away" and that has been an ethic I strive to live by. Reading these pages is an opportunity to refuse to look away–to bear witness to the experience and wisdom and then to take our place in the revolution. "We have nothing to lose but our chains" ~Assata Shakur

Lisa Xochitl Vallejos, PhD
Rocky Mountain Humanistic Counseling and Psychological Association

Rising Voices covers topics relating to social justice, activism, discrimination, and empathy, focusing on the need to speak out and inspire us all to stay woke. This book will impress poetry lovers because the voices are here and now, and real. We all feel the healing power when we are free to share our stories without fear of judgment. Stories are how we humans understand ourselves and each other. One of my greatest teachers (Dr. David Simon) told me that behind every illness there is a love story waiting to be told. If we allow someone to share their story with us, they will eventually reveal where they are stuck in life. Our life is our story, and each one of us has a unique story to tell. I'm grateful for these great activists, authors, and poets who share their soul's talent–making the world better, one poem at a time.

Denise Widner (C-IAYT), Mental Health Counselor candidate

Rising Voices: Poems Toward a Social Justice Revolution

Edited by
Louis Hoffman
Nathaniel Granger, Jr.
Veronica Lac

Rising Voices: Poems Toward a Social Justice Revolution
Edited by Louis Hoffman, Nathaniel Granger, Jr., & Veronica Lac

First published in 2022. University Professors Press. United States.

ISBN (hardcover): 978-1-955737-11-1
ISBN (paperback): 978-1-955737-12-8
ISBN (ebook):   978-1-955737-13-5

University Professors Press
Colorado Springs, CO
www.universityprofessorspress.com

Front Cover Art, "Phases," by Shanah (Leaf) Cooley
Cover Design by Laura Ross

Reprint permissions listed with the poems.

Dedication

For the social justice advocates and activists who have challenged me, and taught me, who have not let me sit with my comfort, who have inspired me, and who have created a better world while knowing that still—*still*—there is so much more work to be done.

   ~ Louis

For those who not only talk the talk but also walk the walk to ensure Liberty and Justice for all. To those committed to making this world a better place than what they found it.

   ~Nathaniel

For those who have learned to quiet their voices, may they rise and be heard loudly, freely, and justly. For all whose voices have helped to lift mine, I am grateful for your invitation to join the call for social justice as we continue to find ways to be heard.

   ~ Veronica

Poetry, Healing, and Growth Series

Stay Awhile: Poetic Narratives on Multiculturalism and Diversity
Louis Hoffman & Nathaniel Granger, Jr. (Eds.)

Capturing Shadows: Poetic Encounters Along the Path of Grief and Loss
Louis Hoffman & Michael Moats (Eds.)

Journey of the Wounded Soul: Poetic Companions for Spiritual Struggles
Louis Hoffman & Steve Fehl (Eds.)

Our Last Walk: Using Poetry for Grieving and Remembering Our Pets
Louis Hoffman, Michael Moats, and Tom Greening (Eds.)

Poems for and about Elders (Revised & Expanded Edition)
Tom Greening

Connoisseurs of Suffering: Poetry for the Journey to Meaning
Jason Dias & Louis Hoffman (Eds.)

Silent Screams: Poetic Journeys Through Addiction & Recovery
Nathaniel Granger, Jr. & Louis Hoffman

Waterfalls of Therapy
Michael Elliott

A Walk with Nature: Poetic Encounters that Nourish the Soul
Michael Moats, Derrick Sebree, Jr., Gina Subia Belton, & Louis Hoffman

Into the Void: An Existential Psychologist Faces Death Through Poetry
Tom Greening

Lullabies & Confessions: Poetic Explorations of Parenting Across the Lifespan
Louis Hoffman & Lisa Xochitl Vallejos

A 21st Century Plague: Poetry from a Pandemic
Elayne Clift

Poetry, Healing, and Growth Series

The ancient healing art of poetry has been used across cultures for thousands of years. In the Poetry, Healing, and Growth book series, the healing and growth-facilitating nature of poetry is explored in depth through books of poetry and scholarship, as well as through practical guides on how to use poetry in the service of healing and growth. Poetry written with an intention to transform suffering into an artistic encounter is often different in process and style from poetry written for art's sake. This series offers engagement with the poetic greats and literary approaches to poetry while also embracing the beauty of fresh, poetic starts and encouraging readers to embark upon their own journey with poetry. Whether you are an advanced poet, avid consumer, or novice to poetry, we are confident you will find something to inspire your thinking on your personal path toward healing and growth.

Series Editors,
Carol Barrett, PhD; Steve Fehl, PsyD; Nathaniel Granger, Jr., PsyD; Tom Greening, PhD; and Louis Hoffman, PhD

Table of Contents

Acknowledgments

First, we want to thank the many talented poets who contributed to this volume. You are inspiring! Many tears were shed while reading through these poems. Participating in a book such as this often entails risk—risk in sharing one's voice and, for some, sharing one's story. The poets were patient as we experienced several delays. We also want to thank the many activists and advocates who have dedicated their lives to social justice work. You are our inspirations for this book. Without these inspiring people, we never would have ventured into this book. Thank you.

***

I (Louis) first would like to thank the many people who had the courage to confront and guide me in my own humble pursuits to contribute to social justice. As Yaqui Martinez noted, "The writer is always a web of relationships... The writer is a we" (Roundtable discussion, COVID and the Givens of Existence Conference, 2021). You are part of this writing, part of my "we." I want to acknowledge "The Boss," Bruce Springsteen, who was the first person to really inspire me toward social justice through his music and poetry. In my youth, his lyrics and music helped me understand the suffering of others and helped me believe that compassion, empathy, and sharing stories can change the world. I want to acknowledge many social justice colleagues/mentors, including Heatherlyn Cleare-Hoffman, Theopia Jackson, Nathaniel Granger, Jr., Lisa Xochitl Vallejos, Veronica Lac, Zonya Johnson, Alan Vaughan, Joel Federman, David St. John, Shawn Rubin, Joy Hoffman, John Hoffman, Joel Vos, and Ian Wickramasekera. There have been many students and former students who, in their willingness to speak up and speak out, have inspired me and pushed me to do more and do better. No doubt, I am a better professor and person because of many students who have been courageous enough to share and teach while they were learning. Thank you. The music, poetry, and scholarly contributions of Rhiannon Giddens have been one of the most profound recent inspirations for me in social justice work. Giddens's songs and many of her talks on YouTube have been steady companions for several years, and particularly while preparing this volume. Finally, I want to acknowledge the most vital inspirations in my life: Heatherlyn, Lakoda, Lukaya, and Lyon. Because of you, every day I think about what I can do to make the world a better place so that maybe you won't have to suffer quite so much injustice. Already, I have witnessed too many of your unnecessary tears and fears. I love you dearly, and rarely does a week pass that I do not shed my own tears thinking about the burden you have to carry that you did not choose. I promise that I will continue to treasure these tears as testimonies of my love for you and motivation to never stop learning, and to never stop fighting to bring about a better world.

***

I (Nathaniel) would like to extend my heartfelt appreciation collectively to all those who continue the tedious and arduous work in social justice—students, professionals, and colleagues, alike. Some who have supported the cause are mothers with children, who cannot do much more than teach their children the importance of the closing stance of our Pledge Allegiance, *"With Liberty and Justice for All"* and lend their voice through poetry. Others are in the trenches, starting and working with grassroots movements toward social change. Yet others are Whites, who advocate for and walk with marginalized groups in the fight for equality. The list is exhaustive and consists of people from all walks of life; however, they share a common respect for human dignity and a synergistic goal in the betterment of society by, as my 2018 Society for Humanistic Psychology Presidential theme denotes, *"Embracing our Fear, Courage, and Love In Pursuit of a Just Community."* Although my inspiration has come from so many human connections, to include you reading this acknowledgement, I would be remiss if I did not acknowledge individually a few who have stood with me as I have tirelessly worked in the arena of Human Services: My family, particularly my wife Areta, who has watched me crash, burn, and rise again and again, only to help try to make this world a better place for others. She has shared in my many tears and late-night conversations on societal ills and mused into the early morning hours on ways to solve them. And Louis Hoffman, my friend-turned-family, whose continued support and undying commitment to social justice has fueled my torch during times when the way seemed hopelessly dark.

***

I (Veronica) want to acknowledge the incredible privilege of being an editor for this book. The poems shared by our contributors felt sacred, raw, inspiring, and heartbreaking. I want to acknowledge my privilege of having the opportunity to join the call for social justice through this particular medium—an academic press for existential–humanistic psychology. I exist as a microscopic part of the greater fight toward social change, a niche within a niche, in the White space of equine-facilitated therapy, surrounded more by animals than humans in my everyday life. But even here, within the small corner of my world, I see the impact of centering conversations about diversity, equity, and inclusion. I am grateful to my students who have risked stepping into this space with me. Most of all, I am thankful for the safe spaces with fellow warriors, allies, and accomplices that I have found to process my own experiences of prejudice and racism, particularly Louis Hoffman, Elizabeth McCorvey, Shannon Knapp, Helena Lee, and Alison McCabe. With you all, I know that I will always have refuge.

Introduction

All the poet can do to-day is warn. That is why the true
Poets must be truthful. (Owen, 2021)

Is it possible, too, that one poet, one pen, and one poem
can change the world? Has not history already answered
that question for us? (Hutchison, 2013)

Why create another book of social justice poetry? After all, there are
other outstanding volumes already in print (c.f., Bush & Meyer, 2013;
Cushway & Warr, 2016; Garner, 2016; Fellner & Young, 2012). We
created this book because we, the editors and the contributors, still
have something to say. We are aware that when it comes to social justice,
there is still much work to be done. Often, as we have had conversations
about social justice and prepared for this book, somewhere in our
conversation one of us said, "There is so much work to be done!" We are
writing to add to the inspiration for social justice and to nurture those
who are now weary and tired from doing this work. We are writing as
witnesses to the pain and suffering that is too prevalent in the world
today. We are writing because in the last several years, racism, which
has never left us, has taken off its mask and spoken up with a renewed
vengeance. We are writing because we know there is a world in need of
healing and growth. We are writing because there are stories and voices
that need to be heard. We are writing because we are still eager to learn
from the stories and perspectives of others. We are writing, too, because
we are poets—we are writers—and this is how we heal ourselves and
nurture our own wounds.

This book began over five years ago and suffered many delays
because life continues to happen even when you have a book to create.
Maybe this delay was a blessing. In recent years, the United States and
much of the world have witnessed so many social justice atrocities. The
murder of George Floyd on May 25, 2020 catalyzed many social justice
activists and movements. Despite the COVID-19 pandemic, people
grabbed their signs and megaphones and took to the streets while
others grabbed their pen and began to write. They spoke out
demanding change. And they spoke out because they needed to get the

pain out. We still need both the pen and the megaphone as we tell these stories. Inaugural Poet, Amanda Gorman (2021), captured the moment in her poem, "The Hill We Climb," highlighting the need for us all to continue the work of those who came before us, and demonstrating the power of activism through poetry.

In this volume we hope to both agitate and to comfort. And, we invite you, the reader, to be uncomfortable. This is part of the work that is needed. The resistance to being uncomfortable has served to protect the privileged and the oppressors.[1] As we reviewed the poems and discussed which poems to include, we often ventured into our own heartbreak and discomfort. Particularly for those of us who have not been historically marginalized, if we are really doing this work, the discomfort should never end. Yet, for those in the midst of these struggles, we also hope to comfort, to help people recognize that they are not alone. We hope to let advocates and activists know that their voices matter as they put their comfort, their safety, and even their lives at risk to create a world that is more just.

Poetry and Activism

Poetry and other forms of art have had a tenuous relationship with activism. Actors, singers, and activists have long used their platforms to make political and social justice statements. In recent years, it has become more common to hear responses such as, "Shut up and play." In one of the more dramatic examples, in 2003 Natalie Maines of the Dixie Chicks (now "The Chicks") received death threats after she made a critical statement about then President George W. Bush at a concert in London, England. Many of their fans and many country radio stations boycotted music by the Dixie Chicks. Repeatedly, Maines and her bandmates were told to "Shut up and sing." Three years later they released the song "Not Ready to Make Nice" (Maguire et al., 2016), which was a response to what Maines and her bandmates went through. As Schorn (2006) notes, the anger in the unapologetic song, "isn't directed at the war or the president—or at their many fans who deserted them. It's about the hatred, and narrow-minded intolerance they encountered for expressing an opinion."

Hutchison (2013) noted that poets also have been discouraged, and

---

[1] It is important to acknowledge, too, that even being able to write this book reflects our privilege. We have time and resources, as well as the advanced educational background that prepared us.

even punished, when engaging in social justice topics. He stated, "cultural arbiters—academia, arts organizations, grant-making foundations, and the vast majority of publishers—prefer to foster the careers of poets who adopt strictly personal and/or theoretical stances in their work" (p. 13). An implicit message is that these artists do not have anything of importance to say; they are merely entertainers and surely not informed on the issues. While this critique may be true in some situations, it is not always accurate. When it comes to social justice, many artists from historically marginalized and oppressed groups have first-hand experience with oppression, as Carol Hanisch (1970) noted in her famous essay, "The personal is political." Echoes of this can also be heard in Marvin Gaye's (1971) famous song, "What's Going On?"

For many artists, engaging in deep empathy is vital to their craft. This is true of performing artists, songwriters, musicians, fiction authors, and poets. Without deep connection with the subject, the art too often falls flat. Artists frequently rely upon often-neglected ways of knowing, such as empathy, emotion, and relationship. The neglect of inclusive ways of knowing contributes to covering over the scars, wounds, and tears of many who have suffered. We reach a deeper understanding when we incorporate diverse ways of knowing (i.e., epistemologies) and recognize that any singular way of knowing is imperfect and insufficient. Through bringing a new vantage and telling stories that have been too often ignored or deliberately silenced, artists help bring a more complete understanding of the topic being considered.

Art itself can be understood as a way of knowing—one that often incorporates and draws upon other ways of knowing. It can be a vital part of sense-making (i.e., making sense of a situation). Gaylie (2007) discussed the use of poetry and film to raise social justice awareness, including how engaging with a film that incorporated images, video, and poetry about war led to creating a "Peace Tree" on a university campus. Gaylie noted,

> The film, the poems, and the action allowed students to examine and channel their uncomfortable reactions, and perhaps encourage others to wonder about the Peace Tree. One of the students later told me that the day we watched the film everything changed; the student teachers moved from observers seeking information...to participants constructing equitable, engaged, informed, globally inspired, peaceful

interaction. (p. 65)

This example illustrates how art can inform while simultaneously inspiring one to action. It is not mere entertainment. Art changes the world.

Examples abound of how poetry helps understand atrocities of the world and bring about change. In one powerful example, Griswold and Murphy (2014) write about the landays of Afghanistan. Landays are short, two-line poems of 22 syllables. The first line is nine syllables, and the second line is 13. These can be easily memorized and used as a way to educate, express, and resist. Most landays are written by women and reflect themes ranging from love to grief to war. Because these are considered to be coming from the collective, they are not attributable to specific individuals, making them a safe way to communicate and to provide resistance. For example, some of the landays speak to the destruction of one's village and home by drones from the United States. Other landays speak to the situation of women in Afghanistan, such as being forced into an arranged marriage with a much older man or dealing with infidelity. Many of these landays contain the power in just 22 syllables to take one's breath away.

During the Cultural Revolution in China, literary works and art that were not deemed supportive of the Communist regime were routinely burned and eliminated. Eventually, ALL art was considered political and therefore banned. The Misty Poets (the leaders of which are commonly identified as Bei Dao, Gu Cheng, Shu Ting, He Don, and Yan Lian) was a group of 20th century poets whose works spoke out against the Cultural Revolution. They were exiled after the Tiananmen Square Protests in 1989. Poetry as political and subversive acts of social activism is universal.

For youth in the United States, slam poetry has become a source of "political engagement and social involvement" (Muhammad & Gonzales, 2016, p. 445). One common intent of slam poetry is to invite the reader to consider the experience of the author. However, slam poetry often is not just expressive of one's experience; it takes into account one's social positions, which makes it activist poetry. Engaging social and political topics often requires the poet to conduct both formal and informal research in preparing the poem. For example, in the "Journey of Brilliance," Aliya J'anai did her research. She identified and incorporated many neglected achievements of people of African descent and connected it with her own personal experience. The mixture of the research, subjectivity, and engagement with social issues creates a powerful experience for the listener or reader.

Maybe the activist potential of poetry is one of the reasons why, as Hutchison (2013) noted, socially and politically engaged poetry has been frowned upon and has lacked support within many of the authority structures such as academic departments, funding sources, and other organizations. As Gradilla (2015) reminds us, "in all ancient societies poetry was seen as the purest and most dangerous form of truth and knowledge" (p. 7). Social justice and activist poetry threaten the status quo and, quite often, is intended to—that is the point! Maher (2019) notes that Plato encouraged the censorship of poets and, more recently, that Trump did not support or renew funding for the National Student Poets Program. Similarly, some politicians who view it as unnecessary or a threat have continually targeted the National Endowment for the Arts. Yes, poetry can be threatening. And this is something that we hope to preserve. Its threat is not that of violence, but persuasion, insight, inspiration, and illuminating the injustices of the world. And this threat can empower and inspire the work of tearing down the structures that maintain injustice.

Narratives that Can Change the World

A normal black child, having grown up with a normal family, will become abnormal at the slightest contact with the white world. (Fanon, 1952/2008, p. 122)

The hope is that well-told stories describing the reality of black and brown lives can help readers to bridge the gap between their worlds and those of others. Engaging stories can help us understand what life is like for others and invite the reader into a new and unfamiliar world. (Delgado & Stefancic, 2017, p. 49)

Stories can oppress as well as liberate. When the stories that are heard are primarily from the dominant or privileged groups of society, they almost inevitably oppress. As the above quote from Fanon (1952/2008) forcefully states, the stories of the dominant group easily can be used to marginalize or pathologize individuals from historically oppressed groups. For example, Ben Carson, when he was the director of Housing and Urban Development, made a statement comparing individuals from Africa who were captured, brought to America, and forced into slavery to immigrants hoping for a better life (Adams, 2017).

While Carson later posted a response to the criticism he received clarifying that he recognized the slave narrative and immigrant narrative were different, it still reflects a historical narrative that tried to portray people who were enslaved as "happy slaves." Many similar narratives have been offered by white people since the beginning of slavery to justify its existence and relieve white people of guilt. Of course, this narrative could only be written by an oppressor.

Similarly, former President Donald Trump repeatedly used the narrative that immigrants from Mexico, Central America, and South America were criminals to further his political agenda (Colvin, 2018). Despite repeated fact checks demonstrating the inaccuracies, including some pointing out that immigrants have a lower crime rate than citizens, Trump persisted with this narrative that long has been used to stoke racism against LatinX individuals (Boak, 2019; Gore, 2019; Haslett, 2019).

During the COVID-19 pandemic, Trump repeatedly blamed China for the virus, including spreading numerous disproven and unproven conspiracy theories about the origins, handling, and spread of the virus (Yam, 2020). Despite the lack of evidence to support his claims, the narrative was effective. The Anti-defamation League (2020) reported an 85% increase in conspiracy theories and anti-Asian rhetoric on Twitter after Trump was diagnosed with COVID-19. The implications of the anti-Asian prejudice is reflected in "With One Look" by Lac, in which she states:

> From behind your mask, you tried in vain
> to hide the fact you moved
> away, pulling yourself
> to a safer distance, away from
> me, this Asian woman's face
> just in case, just in case, just in case
> I might carry disease

While stories can cause harm, they can also bring about change. In response to these narratives that harm groups of people based upon their social position(s), Delgado and Stefancic (2017) suggest that we can "use counterstories to challenge, displace, or mock these pernicious narratives and beliefs" (p. 50). But stories can do more than counter the distorted, prejudicial stores. They can help provide a narrative that deepens understanding and empathy. Furthermore, these stories can be a self-affirmation of one's experience and help to demonstrate that one is not alone.

In Jennifer O'Neill's poem "Angry. Black. Woman.," she addresses the narrative of the strong black woman and angry black woman. The narrative of the strong black woman may appear to some as a compliment; however, there are more nefarious connotations with this portrayal. For example, the label of being a strong black woman or strong black man has been connected with the belief that black people do not experience as much pain or have higher tolerances of pain (Hoffman, Trawalter, et al., 2016). It can be used as a justification for the common reality of black people being prescribed less medication for their pain. Related to the strong black woman portrayal is the idea of being an angry black woman—another common stereotype. In her poem, O'Neill affirms and contextualizes her anger in the challenges and the suffering she faces. She makes the anger human. Too often in society, the anger of white individuals is humanized, while the anger of black, indigenous, and people of color (BIPOC) individuals is pathologized. In the affirmative telling of her story, O'Neill powerfully challenges these damaging characterizations of black women.

Granger's "The Brightest Smile" tells the story of his interaction with a veteran experiencing homelessness. The poem reflects Granger's empathy and calls the reader to empathy as well. Too often, people experiencing homelessness face multiple levels of dehumanization, including a lack of reciprocity and acknowledgment of being a fellow human deserving of being treated with dignity. Rarely do people show interest in their story; instead, the people experiencing homelessness are treated as a problem or nuisance. At best, they may be treated with pity but rarely do these suffering souls receive the treatment of dignity. In Granger's poem, he reflects empathy, not just pity. More than that, it witnesses the treatment of this individual with reciprocity and dignity, even in just noticing and valuing the smile of the veteran experiencing homelessness.

Stories are important in the development of empathy, which can be a vital tool for social justice work when not idealized or simplified. Delgado and Stefancic (2017) note, "One premise of legal storytellers is that members of this country's dominant racial group cannot easily grasp what it is like to be nonwhite." Hoffman and Granger (2015) discuss that the motivation for *Stay Awhile: Poetic Narratives on Multiculturalism and Diversity*—a previous volume in the Poetry, Healing, and Growth Series—was rooted in the belief that stories often can make an impact where other forms of discourse and debate fail. Stories push for understanding of the other person's experience and sometimes these stories, through the empathy and understanding they bring about, can produce change. Yet, as Delgado and Stefancic (2017) note, it is important not to idealize empathy. They define the *empathetic fallacy* as the "mistaken belief that sweeping social reform can be accomplished through speech and incremental victories within the system" (p. 173). This definition is based on a limited understanding of empathy, and we may question whether that is really empathy. However, their criticism is still important. While we deeply believe in the power and potential of stories and empathy—as do Delgado and Stefancic—we also recognize that this, alone, is not enough

In "Evolve," Joy Hoffman shares her experiences of racism as an Asian woman, ranging from being tokenized to being viewed as a "model minority," to being feared because of COVID-19. Yet, she continues. The poem is not just a retelling of racism, but also a formidable affirming of herself and her culture. In the second to last stanza, she writes,

> I AM the strength of my ancestors,
> The joy of community,
> The power of solidarity,
> The healing in my soul,
> And compassion of my heart.

These lines affirm who she is as a person beyond the stereotypes projected upon her. In concluding, she also uses her story to point to hope:

> After the grief,
> The fear,
> The rage,
> And exhaustion,
> I am always,
> Quite surprisingly,
> Hopeful.

Yes, there is still hope. Despite all changes that are needed, despite the suffering that surrounds, despite the systemic barriers to equity, there is a place for hope. This is not a naive hope that brushes off the reality that Joy Hoffman discusses; it is an earned hope that acknowledges the very real challenges of the world.

Reclaiming History

Steve King, in an interview with Chris Hayes on MSNBC, noted,

> I'd ask you to go back through history and figure out, where are these contributions that have been made by these other categories of people (i.e., nonwhite) that you're talking about, where did any other subgroup of people contribute more to civilization? (Petroski, 2016)

King, in his limited and distorted understanding of history, is not the only person to believe that BIPOC individuals have not made substantial contributions to advancements in the world. Too often, our current education system favors a presentation of history that focuses on the contributions of Euro-Americans while neglecting many contributions of BIPOC individuals.

In the opening poem of this volume, Aliya J'anai corrects the false beliefs of Steve King and so many others who only know the comfortable history they have been taught. She chronicles many—though certainly not all—contributions of individuals from Africa or of African descent, ranging from math and science to the Super Soaker. To cover all the contributions would require an epic poem that could be a book, or rather volumes of books, of its own.

The correcting of histories like Steve King's is one important aspect of social justice work. The arts can play a vital role in correcting this history. The folk/bluegrass singer Rhiannon Giddens provides many examples of this social justice work in her lyrics as well as her discussion of the history of many genres of music in the United States. In her album, *Freedom Highway*, Giddens (2017) shares many lyrical slave stories. For example, the powerful song *Julie* tells the story of a woman, Julie, who was enslaved. The woman who enslaved her begs for Julie's help as the soldiers come. Like Steve King, the woman who enslaved Julie seems completely unaware of Julie's experience until Julie, who denies the woman's pleas, shares her side of the story.

Elsewhere, Giddens (2018; see also Davidson, 2019) challenges the white-washed history of American music. She demonstrates how many "American" instruments and musical styles began with instruments designed by people kidnapped from Africa and brought to the Caribbean and Americas. Many of these early instruments were designed to resemble or replicate instruments from Africa. Giddens shows how nearly all—or maybe all—"American" music has roots in

Africa.

The music artist Common (2000) works to correct the weaponized history of Assata Shakur in his song, "A Song for Assata." Assata has been described as the mother of the Black Panthers. She was involved with the Black Panther movement and had been arrested many times (Shakur, 1987). Most of these charges were dismissed due to a lack of evidence. Prior to her arrest that led to her conviction, she was being closely tracked by the FBI. In 1977, she was convicted related to a shooting despite evidence that she had already been shot with her hands up and could not have pulled the trigger. In 1979 Shakur escaped from prison and in 1984 was granted asylum in Cuba, where she has lived since. As recently as 2017, then president Donald Trump continued to demand that Assata Shakur, who was 70-years old at the time, be extradited to the United States. Common, as a popular musical artist, used his art and his platform to retell Shakur's story in a voice other than that of her oppressors.

Before history was an academic discipline, it was used to preserve the accounts of what happened, whether they were literal or mythic histories. Today, poetry and other forms of art can preserve history and correct mis-told histories. In the "Ballad of Sandra Bland" in this volume, Edgren tells the story of a more contemporary victim of mis-told history. As Edgren notes, "they tried to call her crazy." Yet, the evidence does not fit the picture painted of Sandra Bland. The construction of a narrative, a history that serves the oppressor has long been used in the service of justifying oppression. If we are going to put an end to oppression, it is critical to dismantle the tools of oppression, such as histories told only by the oppressor. J'anai, Giddens, Common, and Edgren are not just creating art; they are doing the hard work of social justice.

Social Justice Activism's Role in Social and Personal Healing

> Poetry means a protest that no one can take away from me, a therapist no money could buy, a story no one else could tell... I think that every poem is a piece of rebellion and activism. (Contreras-Montesano, as quote in Maher, 2019)

Rhiannon Giddens (2016), in discussing how she wrote the song "At the Purchaser's Option," noted that it began as she read an advertisement about people who were enslaved and being sold at an auction. After describing the mother, it mentioned a nine-month-old baby that was "at the purchaser's option." She went on to say, "And it just kind of made me... really sad. And the way that I deal with all the stuff inside is I write" (Giddens, 2016). Giddens has written a number of songs that deal with painful aspects of history. But they are not just history for those who have come from a former place in time. This history still has a lived presence in today's world. It is not something that we can just get over.

Giddens's comment about writing to process and deal with painful emotions is supported by extensive research (Frattaroli, 2006; Pavlacic et al., 2019; Pennebaker & Smyth, 2016; Travagin et al., 2015; van Emmerik et al., 2013). Although the research is not as extensive, these benefits also have been found specifically with poetry (Brillantes-Evangelista, 2013; Chan, 2003; Daboui et al, 2018; Jahanpour et al., 2019). There are various mechanisms related to poetry and expressive writing that may contribute to its benefits, including expressing and processing emotions, sense making, meaning making, facilitating connection with others, and promoting self-affirmation.

Social justice advocacy and activism also can be healing. L. Hoffman and colleagues (2016) noted that the Black Lives Matter and other contemporary protest movements serve various functions, including promoting social change while contributing to individual and collective healing. Similar to poetry, activism can facilitate connection and a realization that one is not alone, meaning making, emotional expression, and a sense of hope. Activism, too, can promote communal healing as well as personal healing.

While the healing dimensions of activism are important, they do not replace the need for social and systemic change. Rather, activism helps sustain individuals, groups, and communities seeking such change. We need both personal healing and collective/systemic change.

Claiming Meaning

The work of social justice is hard. Many who do this work are asked why they choose to engage in something that is so difficult and so exhausting. There are many answers to this question, including that for many the hardness is a lived reality whether they engage directly in social justice work or not.

Viktor Frankl (1984), who endured the concentration camps of Nazi Germany, wrote extensively about the transformative power of meaning. Hoffman, Granger et al. (2016), drawing in part from Frankl, advocated that activism is one way to create meaning that can help to transform the suffering of racial oppression and injustice. It does not take away the suffering or the injustice, but it can begin to transform aspects of the suffering as one works to address the injustice.

The arts are a powerful way to claim meaning in the face of injustice. This meaning can sustain and invigorate individuals who are trying to change unjust realities in the world. And often, it is contagious. When others witness the meaning being created, they are drawn toward it.

It is critical to recognize that personal meaning alone is not sufficient. While this can help one sustain and energize the social justice work one is engaged with, it is important to push further toward collective meanings and systemic changes that make people's lives better.

The title of this book, *Raising Voices*, intends to be representative of the drive for meaning and change. We hope the reader can feel the energy of this title—feel the energy of speaking up from the experience of pain, suffering, and oppression toward change. We hope, too, that you feel this in the poems within the book.

Social Construction and Social Justice

It wasn't until after college that I started really learning about the fallacious farce that is race. The made-up BS that has been handed us with every meal like a disgusting after dinner mint that nobody wants but everybody eats anyway. It's incredible to think how something that is anti-science, anti-intellect, and clearly supports a destructive ultra-violent colonial capitalism imbues our every waking moment in America whether we are aware of it or not. (Giddens, 2021)

The social construction of race maintains that there is no such thing as race in a biological sense; rather, race is a socially constructed entity. Furthermore, it can be maintained that race was constructed by white individuals for the benefit of white people. The construction of race has varied over time. Bridges (2019) notes that some groups—such as Italians and Irish—who are now considered white, were not always considered so. The construction of race often centered around labeling some groups as inferior and using this to justify behavior toward them, such as enslaving them or not affording these groups certain rights given to others.

Because the construction of race is fluid, it often changes based on what benefits white people. In the 2016 elections, it became advantageous for some politicians to present Latinx refugees from Central and South America as criminals. The fear and anger associated with this helped energize many to support various candidates running for office. As a consequence, many Latinx Americans, immigrants, and refugees experienced increased racism. In 2020 during the COVID-19 pandemic, it became advantageous to blame China for the virus. This covered over the many failures within the United States government and leadership in addressing the virus. The result, however, was many Asian Americans becoming the target of increased racism. During this period, hate crimes against Asian Americans, immigrants, and refugees rose dramatically.

Because constructions of race tend to change based upon the benefits of white people, "progress" often occurs when it benefits white people, which is called *interest convergence*. Interest convergence can be understood in the context of white privilege. Phillips and Lowrey (2018) note that the two primary resistances to white privilege awareness are the investment in being seen as a good person and opposition to giving up the benefits of white privilege. Many white people will support social justice efforts that raise up BIPOC individuals but end their support when it means giving up their unearned benefits or privilege. Until white people are willing to give up their unearned privileges, progress will remain limited and equity will remain elusive.

Maintaining that race is socially constructed does not, however, mean that there are not very real implications for what is identified as race. In other words, the construction of race has real world consequences and realities even if it is something that would not exist were it not constructed by human beings. Genetically, human beings share 99% of the same genes (Bridges, 2019). Furthermore, there is more within-group differences than between-group differences. Yet, the different treatment of people based upon superficial characteristics such as skin color, hair texture, and facial structure is real.

Intersectionality

Intersectionality is a complex term that evolved overtime. Kimberlé Crenshaw (1989) originally defined this term focusing particularly on the intersectionality of being black and being a woman. Being both black and a woman has implications for one's identity and how one is treated in the world. Over time, this term has evolved to be used to refer to many types of intersectionality, such as gender, sexual identity, race, ability, and other aspects of how one is perceived and identified. The editors and authors of this book all write from particular intersections of identity. Veronica is a British Asian woman, born in Hong Kong under colonial rule, and holds permanent residence status in the United States. Nathaniel is a black man from Chicago who grew up in poverty before entering the military and later obtaining his doctorate degree. Louis is a white male of a privileged background who married a black woman from the Bahamas and has three multiracial children. For each of us, these intersections influence how we see and experience the world. They influence, too, how the world sees and treats us. Similarly, each poet is writing from their own intersection that influenced the voice that comes through in their poem.

Individuals often get lost in the intersections. Crenshaw (1989) described the case of a black women who was being discriminated against. Because the employer hired and promoted black men, it was maintained that racism was not a valid argument. Because other women were hired and promoted, the argument of sexism was deemed invalid. The intersections can serve to hide prejudice and discrimination where it does, in reality, exist.

Intersectionality is not merely the sum of different forms of discrimination (Bridges, 2019). In Crenshaw's example, the black woman's experience of discrimination is not equivalent to racism from being black plus sexism from being a woman. There is something unique to the experience of being a black woman that is different than the sum of racism and sexism. If we want to understand the unique experiences of people, it is necessary to understand the contributions of intersectionality as well as the experiences of racism, sexism, homophobia, and other forms of prejudice and discrimination.

Critical Race Theories

> It is a common saying nowadays that racism is a plague of humanity. But we must not content ourselves with such a phrase. We must tirelessly look for the repercussions of racism at all levels of sociability. (Fanon, 1964/1967)

Critical Race Theory (CRT) is foundational for much contemporary social justice work. However, it would be more appropriate to refer to critical race theories (Bridges, 2019). CRT is not a unitary theory and, in ways, is not so much a theory as a tool or lens. Various CRT scholars have maintained that people identifying with CRT do not agree on its primary foundations, which are generally identified as between four to eight assumptions (Bridges, 2019; Delgado & Stefancic, 2017). In general, a primary focus of CRT is to understand the ongoing existence and impact of racism in the United States following the civil rights movement. This is not to denigrate the civil rights movement or leaders, but rather to acknowledge that despite what was accomplished, racism is still alive and well in the United States.

CRT originated out of legal studies (Bridges, 2019; Delgado & Stefancic, 2017); however, over time it has evolved to find a presence in many different disciplines, including the social sciences. Additionally, there are many perspectives on CRT, such as Islamic and Latinx Critical Race theories. As CRT has developed, it has evolved and diversified, as any good, robust theory should.

Drawing from Delgado and Stefancic (2017) and Bridges (2019), we identify the following primary principles of CRT, many of which are themes already discussed in this chapter:

1. Race is a social construction, not a biological entity (Bridges, 2019; Delgado & Stefancic, 2017).
2. Racial problems or racism is normal in the United States and much of the world (Bridges, 2019; Delgado & Stefancic, 2017). This means that the reality of racism is pervasive, and it is more common for race to play a role in various aspects of society than for it not to have an influence.
3. Traditional liberal understandings of racism have limitations (Bridges, 2019; Delgado & Stefancic, 2017). This is a primary reason why liberal attempts to address racism after the civil rights movements have failed to end the problem of race.
4. Limited incentive for white people, particularly "white elites," provides a barrier to eradicating racism (Delgado & Stefancic, 2017). Sometimes called "interest convergence" (p. 9), history has shown that typically a majority of white individuals do not become interested in addressing the problems associated with race until there is some benefit for them.
5. White society racializes BIPOC individuals at different times and in different contexts (Delgado & Stefancic, 2017). Often, this is based on what is most advantageous for white people at the current time.
6. When considering issues of race, it is important to consider intersectionality (Delgado & Stefancic, 2017).

7. CRT believes that scholarship must not be limited to the development of ideas and theories but rather should be applied (Bridges, 2019).

8. BIPOC individuals have unique experiences and stories to tell (Delgado & Stefancic, 2017). Noted Delgado and Stefancic, "the voice-of-color thesis holds that because of their different histories and experiences with oppression, black, American Indian, Asian, and Latino writers and thinkers may be able to communicate to their white counterparts matters that the whites are unlikely to know" (p. 11). This last principle is highly relevant to the motivation for the current book.

It can be noted that almost all, or arguably all, of these principles are not unique to CRT, which has just incorporated them and formed a particular way of utilizing them to understand the continued existence of racism.

These principles are starkly different from how CRT is frequently presented in contemporary media. For example, it is commonly purported that CRT says white people are bad or guilty by nature; however, this contradicts the principle that race is a social construction. Guilt is a natural experience associated with white identity development. As white people learn what other white people have done and the implications of this, and as they learn about white privilege, it is natural to have some experiences of feeling guilty. However, to project the cause of this guilt on CRT is a product of a lack of understanding and/or self-awareness rather than reflective of a foundational idea or intent of CRT.

Similarly, CRT is frequently accused of being Marxist. There are numerous problems with this. First and foremost, it is likely that this is often said as a blatant attempt to associate CRT with socialism or communism. In many ways, this is a re-emergence of McCarthyism[2] in new clothing. Like McCarthyism, it reflects an unsophisticated and simplistic understanding of socialism that tries to implicitly connect it with communism. While there are CRT scholars who are Marxists or

---

[2] McCarthyism is a term coined by Herbert Block in an editorial cartoon (Riggs, 2015). It refers to tactics used by Senator Joseph McCarthy in which he baselessly claimed to identify 205 individuals in the State Department as communists. It was part of what has been termed the "Red Scare," which fomented public fears and hysteria about the spread of communism. McCarthyism can be understood as using baseless claims of people being communists or un-American to stir up dissent against them, generally in order to seek some political or other gain.

socialists, this does not make CRT Marxist any more than it makes an entire faculty at a university Marxist because one faculty member identifies as Marxist. Furthermore, a Marxist analytical lens may be used to better understand aspects of race in the United States *without* making the entire theory Marxist. Accusing CRT of being Marxist is a simplistic attack that reflects a lack of understanding of CRT and Marxism or a blatant attempt to defame this theory.[3]

The attacks on CRT (and diversity training) that were elevated and intensified in 2020 and 2021 provide an important case example of the difficulties in conversations about race. The defensiveness and fragility of white individuals worked to redirect the conversation to problems that do not exist. In some ways, taking three paragraphs to respond to the often ridiculous criticisms of CRT is arguably playing into the problem. However, clarification becomes necessary when the basic understanding of CRT is so confused because the voices of people misrepresenting CRT become louder and more prevalent in public discourse than the voices of CRT scholars and advocates.

There also are legitimate critiques of CRT from within the social justice movement. For example, some argue that CRT is theoretical and therefore does not make a significant impact toward social justice. Also, some criticize the focus on language that is often part of CRT, concerned that it focuses on individual experiences of racism instead of addressing the systemic issues. However, this critique does not fit all scholarship in CRT. From a social justice perspective, it is important to engage in critiques of CRT while also examining how it benefits and supports the work of social justice. We believe there are many benefits to drawing from CRT when doing social justice work.

Two of the poems in this volume were written at the same workshop. At this workshop, Nathaniel Granger performed the poem "Bid 'em In," which was originally written and performed by Oscar Brown.[4] This poem is a story of a woman being sold on the auction block. After the powerful performance of this poem, Granger asked for the participants to write a poem in the voice of one of the characters. Two poems, "The Auctioneer" and "The Auctioneer's Unconscious," were written in the voice of the auctioneer. The auctioneer block is one of the most powerful symbols in the history of the United States. It is a symbol of colonization, of slavery, of pain and suffering, and so much

---

[3] To be clear, we are not suggesting that Marxism or being a Marxists is a bad in itself; rather, we are clarifying that CRT is not Marxist and that the critiques of it as Marxist are a simplistic tactic often intended to draw upon the fears of people to defame CRT.
[4] Lyrics available at https://genius.com/Oscar-brown-jr-bid-em-in-lyrics

more.

Writing in the voice of the auctioneer, and any associated empathy or understanding, is not intending to justify the auctioneer's participation in the selling of others. Nothing justifies being involved with such a horrific scene—including distancing it with history. These poems reflect similar themes, including the systemic issues that influence this decision. Burrell writes,

> The only job I've had in my life
> Handed down to me from my Dad
> I preferred to get an education
> But I had to put food on the table for the kids

Rather than suggesting this exonerates the auctioneer, these poems highlight that both personal and systemic responsibility are relevant. Taking into account the social does not eliminate the personal. CRT focuses primarily on systemic and institutional racism. Through emphasizing the collective and systemic responsibility, CRT is not suggesting that individuals should not be held responsible. Rather, CRT is noting that if we only focus on individual racists, specific acts of racism, and instances of racial microaggressions instead of systems of oppression, we fall short.

Jennifer K. Yancy's poem, "I Charge Thee," can be seen as a poetic embodiment of CRT. In the poem, Yancy details many of the common individual and institutional forms of racism that pervade the lives of BIPOC individuals. The poem concludes, proclaiming,

> The American dream has given us PTSD
> And your haughtiness will be the ruination of civilization

This conclusion highlights the consequences (i.e., PTSD) of the history of racism for people of color as well as for all people, including white individuals (i.e., the ruination of a civilization). This is an important connection. Too often it is believed that racism only hurts BIPOC individuals. But this is not true; racism harms everyone.

The Hard and Soft Edges of Social Justice

Social justice work is complex and, in itself, diverse. There is no one way to do social justice work. In this volume, we hope that you see both the hard edges and the soft edges—the anger and the tears, the proclamations and the empathetic ear. Both these edges are needed. Both can be part of systemic change, and both can be part of the healing and self-care needed along the way to this change.

We can see the hard edge in Granger's poem "Call for the Question," in which he delineates many of the social problems that desperately need attention. Granger calls attention to homelessness, rape, child abuse, addiction, poverty, and much more. We see the hard edge, too, in Sean Murphy's confronting of an America:

> Your America
> is not Me.
> Your History
> is not My story.

It is common to hear statements such as, "I just wish they wouldn't disrupt traffic when they protest" and "Why can't they just go through more 'appropriate' channels to advocate for change?" These comments are naïve. Those who have been watching and listening know that the efforts for systemic change to address racism and other social justice issues through "appropriate channels" such as the courts and legal system, have been ongoing for over 100 years! Yet, the problems persist. When change spans generations, the calls for patience ring hallow. Too often, some type of agitating is needed for people to become aware of the issues and what has already been done to seek this change. If you have not been watching or listening closely enough to be aware of these efforts, then you have not earned the right to critique those who are seeking change in a manner that may bring some discomfort. If you have been aware and not done your part to bring about change, then you have the right to ask others to be patient in their suffering and oppression.

A few examples can help illustrate the necessity of the need for the hard edges of social justice. Ahmaud Arbery, a black man, was pursued then shot and killed by armed white men who followed him while he was jogging (Griffith, 2020). It was not until more than a month after the incident and a third prosecutor taking over the case that progress was made toward holding the killers accountable. Without the outcry and protests, it is likely that charges never would have been filed. The protests worked. A second example is that of Elijah McClain, who died on August 30, 2019 after being placed in a carotid hold by a police officer (Andone, 2020). Following the initial investigation, the officers were not indicted, despite many protests. After Georgy Floyd's murder in 2020, the protests for McClain gained renewed momentum. This momentum continued for over a year until in early September 2021—over two years after McClain's death—when the officers involved and two paramedics were indicted. While it is still undetermined what the results of the indictment will be, there is finally some progress. Once again, however, it is unlikely that the officers and paramedics would ever have been indicted without the ongoing protests.

Confrontation often is necessary to expose the problem. Rarely, however, does confrontation alone resolve the issue. In so many individual cases—including Ahmaud Arbery, George Floyd, Sandra Bland, and Elijah McClain—protests have worked. However, if these do not translate into systemic changes, it is likely that the injustices will continue. More is needed. Often the hard and soft edges of social justice need to work in collaboration for the systemic changes to be realized.

The soft edges of social justice work help to advance empathy, understanding, and compassion that begin to change the hearts and opinions of the masses. Without such change, the problems will persist. Often, confrontation is a needed first step to illuminate the problem. Once the problem is illuminated and recognized, there is the possibility for conversations that can lead to deeper change.

A word of caution is important, though. In talking about empathy, we are not advocating that people who have been oppressed and victims of racism should try to be empathetic with the people who have done harm. This may not be safe and open the individual to more harm. We are advocating for cultivating empathy for people who have been marginalized and oppressed.

It is important to recognize that soft edges of social justice work are not always successful, and certainly they will never reach all people. Some individuals are too entrenched in homophobia, racism, Islamophobia, and other forms of oppressive beliefs and systems to be easily reached. No social justice strategy will be able to reach everyone. And no social justice strategy will be successful in every situation. We need varied strategies and sustained effort from both the hard and soft edges of social justice.

Hope

> ...hope cannot be said to exist, nor can it be said not to exist. It is just like the roads across the earth. For actually the earth had no roads to begin with, but when many men pass one way, a road is made. (Lu Xun, 1959,

p. 101)

Hope is vital to social justice work; however, it cannot be a naïve hope. It must be a hope rooted in the courage to face the world honestly. Yet, facing the world directly can all too easily blot out hope when recognizing all the unnecessary suffering that exists. This is part of the paradoxical work of social justice.

Lu Xun (1961) wrote:

> The world is changing from day to day; it is high time for our writers to take off their masks, look frankly, keenly, and boldly at life, and write about real flesh and blood. It is high time for a brand-new arena for literature, high time for some bold fighters to charge headlong into battle! (p. 203)

It may seem a strange place to start the search for hope through facing the bleak realities. Yet, if hope is to be authentic it must begin with being honest about the human condition. Hope rooted in the denial of reality or distortions of the situation not only lacks power but has the potential to do harm.

For example, in sharing concerns about the realities that LGBTQIA+ and BIPOC youth experience, it is common to hear hopeful platitudes about how it is getting better and may not impact these youth. For friends and family of these youth, or the youth themselves, these can feel like daggers in the heart, especially when the platitudes come from friends and family. While the intentions are good, when the realities are not taken seriously, hopeful platitudes are experienced as superficial compassion or naïve optimism. What is needed is a deep compassion and empathy that goes beyond superficial hope to a journeying with. When one journeys with someone who is suffering instead of encouraging from the sidelines, the view is different. The pervasive pains from microaggressions, systemic racism, and other forms of oppression become more evident. The need for change can no longer be denied. Journeying is more effective in seeking real change.

When the change needed is systemic and social on a grand scale, the only sustainable hope is rooted in a community seeking change. No one person can bring about the change; we need a community. While we may be able to see some hope in change that has occurred, this is easily wiped out by the recognition that so many changes have not sustained and have not eradicated the problems. We often witnessed some regression in areas where progress was once made. Over a 100 years of progress has left us not just short, but *far short*. At this rate, it will take many generations, and many lifetimes, before we begin to get anywhere close to the success that is needed. We need more than the hope rooted in the incremental progress of the past. We need a hope rooted in a community committed to tearing down the systems of oppression. It is our aim that this book will help form, support, nurture, encourage, and inspire such a community.

Conclusion

The refrain of this book could be seen as, "There is so much work to be done." It can easily become overwhelming when looking at all the problems that need to be addressed. For some, reading this book may bring a sense of weariness at the reality of the world. But we are optimistic that there may be some hope in finding a community of social justice and activist poets that are ready to grab their pen and megaphone and get to work.

We cannot do it all. No one person can address all the social justice challenges effectively. If we try, we may find ourselves unable to maintain adequate depth of awareness of the issues we are fighting for. Or we may find that we do not have the energy to sustain. No one has to do it all, but we are all called to do our part. And not just to do our part within what is comfortable or easy. Rather, we are called to push ourselves, but not to the point of depletion.

We hope this book may help you find your voice, so that we can collectively raise our voices. We hope, too, that it may be a form of self-care that can nurture, inspire, and make you feel less alone.

References

Adams, C. (2017, March 7). Ben Carson faces backlash after saying slaves were 'immigrants' who came to the U.S. for 'better opportunities.' *People*. Retrieved from https://people.com/politics/ben-carson-backlash-slaves-immigrants-hud/.

Andone, D. (2020, August 24). Elijah McClain died after a police encounter almost one year ago. Here's what happened since. *CNN*. Retrieved from https://www.cnn.com/2020/08/24/us/elijah-mcclain-one-year/index.html

Antidefamation League (2020, October 8). *At the extremes: The 2020 election and American extremism* (Part 3). Retrieved from https://www.adl.org/blog/at-the-extremes-the-2020-election-and-american-extremism-part-3

Boak, J. (2019, February 8). AP fact check: Trump plays on immigration myths. *Public Broadcasting Station (PBS)*. Retrieved from https://www.pbs.org/newshour/politics/ap-fact-check-trump-plays-on-immigration-myths

Bridges, K. M. (2019). *Critical race theory: A primer*. Foundation Press.

Brillantes-Evangelista, G. (2013). An evaluation of visual arts and poetry as therapeutic interventions with abused adolescents. *The Arts in Psychotherapy, 40,* 71–84. http://dx.doi.org/10.1016/j.aip.2012.11.005

Bush, G., & Meyer, R. (Eds.). (2013). *Indivisible: Poems for social justice.* Norwood House Press.

Chan, Z. C. Y. (2003). Poetry writing: A therapeutic means for a social work doctoral student in the process of study. *Journal of Poetry Therapy, 16,* 5–17. https://doi.org/10.1080/0889367031000147995

Common (2000, January 1). A song for Assata. *In Like Water for Chocolate.* https://music.apple.com/us/album/like-water-for-chocolate/1440720260

Colvin, J. (2018, February 7). Trump continues to cast some immigrants as criminals. *Associated Press.* Retrieved from https://apnews.com/article/immigration-north-america-donald-trump-gangs-ap-top-news-a4f02d2b6625439cb1ec53186c466acd

Crenshaw, K. (1989). Demarginalizing the intersection of race and sex: A black feminist critique of antidiscrimination doctrine. *University of Chicago Legal Forum, 1,* 139–167.

Cushway, P., & Warr, M. (Eds.) (2016). *Of poetry and protest: From Emmett Till to Trayvon Martin.* Norton & Company.

Daboui, P., Janbabai, G., & Moradi, S. (2018). Hope and mood improvement in women with breast cancer using group poetry therapy: A questionnaire-based before–after study. *Journal of Poetry Therapy, 31,* 165–172. https://doi.org/10.1080/08893675.2018.1467822

Davidson, J. (2019, March). Rhiannon Giddens 21st-century sound has a long history. *Smithsonian Magazine.* Retrieved from https://www.smithsonianmag.com/arts-culture/rhiannon-giddens-american-music-history-21st-century-sound-180971449/

Delgado, R., & Stefancic, J. (2017). *Critical race theory: An introduction* (3rd ed.). New York University Press.

Fanon, F. (1967). *Toward the African revolution* (H. Chevalier, Trans.). Grove Press. (Original work published in 1964)

Fanon, F. (2008). *Black faces, white masks.* (R. Philcox, Trans.). Grove Press. (Original work published in 1952).

Fellner, S., & Young, P. E. (Eds.). (2012). *Love rise up: An anthology. Poems of social justice, protest and hope.* Benu Press.

Frankl, V. E. (1984). *Man's search for meaning* (3rd ed.). Simon & Schuster.

Frattaroli, J. (2006). Experimental disclosure and its moderators: A meta-analysis. *Psychological Bulletin, 132,* 823–865. https://doi.org/10.1037/0033-2909.132.6.823

Gaye, M. (1971) What's going on? In *What's going on?* https://music.apple.com/us/album/whats-going-on/1538081586

Gaylie, V. (2007). Raising awareness of social justice and war through film and poetry. *Radical Teacher, 79,* 65.

Garner, E. (Ed.). (2016). *Of poetry and protest: From Emmett Till to Trayvon Martin.* Norton.

Giddens, R. (2016). At the purchaser's option: Rhiannon Giddens at Augusta Vocal Week 2016. Retrieved from https://www.youtube.com /watch?v=DVrTf5yOW5s

Giddens, R. (2017). *Freedom highway.* Nonesuch Records. https://music.apple.com/us/album/freedom-highway/1179556528

Giddens, R. (2018). *How Rhiannon Giddens reconstructs black pain with the banjo.* Interview with Michel Martin. Retrieved from https://www.npr.org/2018/04/22/604356508/how-rhiannon-giddens-reconstructs-black-pain-with-the-banjo

Giddens, R. (2021). *To balance on bridges* (Words+Music; Audio Book). Audible.

Gore, D. (2019, February 26). Trump's misdirection on "criminal aliens." *Factcheck.org.* Retrieved from https://www.factcheck.org/2019/02/ trumps-misdirection-on-criminal-aliens/

Gorman, A. (2021). *The hill we climb.* Viking.

Griffith, J. (2020, May 11). Ahmaud Arbery shooting: A timeline of the case. *NBC News.* Retrieved from https://www.nbcnews.com/news/us-news/ahmaud-arbery-shooting-timeline-case-n1204306

Griswold, E., & Murphy, S. (2014). *I am the beggar of the world: Landays from contemporary Afghanistan.* Farrar, Straus, and Giroux.

Gradilla, J. (2015). Foreword. In L. Hoffman & N. Granger, Jr. (Eds.), *Stay awhile: Poetic narratives on multiculturalism and diversity* (pp. 7–8). University Professors Press.

Hanisch, C. (1970). *The personal is political.* Retrieved from http://www.carolhanisch.org/Chwritings/PersonalIsPol.pdf

Haslett, C. (2019, January 15). Fact check: Trump's claim on undocumented immigrant crime rates. Here's what the numbers show. *ABC News.* Retrieved from https://abcnews.go.com/Politics/fact-check-trumps-claims-illegal-immigrant-crime-rates/story?id=60311860

Hoffman, K. M., Trawalter, S. Axt, J. R., & Oliver, M. N. (2016). Racial bias in pain assessment and treatment recommendations, and false beliefs about biological differences between blacks and whites. *PNAS, 113,* 4296–4301. https://doi.org/10.1073/pnas.1516047113

Hoffman, L., & Granger, N. (2015). Stay awhile: Poetic narratives on multiculturalism and diversity. University Professors Press.

Hoffman, L., Granger, N. Jr., Vallejos, L., & Moats, M. (2016). An existential–humanistic perspective on Black Lives Matter and contemporary protest movements. *Journal of Humanistic Psychology, 56,* 595–611. https://doi.org/10.1177/0022167816652273

Hutchinson, J. (2013). Foreword. In J. Hutchison & A. L. Watson (Eds.), *Malala: Poems for Malala Yousafzai* (pp. 11–14). Futurecycle Press.

Jahanpour, F., Armmoon, B., Mozafari, N., Motamed, N., Poor, D. I., & Mirzaee, S. (2019). The comparison of the effect of poetry therapy on anxiety and post-traumatic stress disorders in patients with myocardial infarction. *Journal of Poetry Therapy, 32*, 214–222. https://doi.org/10.1080/08893675.2019.1639884

Lu Xun (1959). My old home. In Y. Xianyi & G. Yang (Eds. & Trans.), *Lu Xun: Selected works* (Vol. 1; pp. 90–101). Foreign Language Press.

Lu Xun (1961). On looking facts in the face. In Y. Xianyi & G. Yang (Eds. & Trans.), *Lu Xun: Selected works* (Vol. 2; pp. 198–204). Foreign Language Press.

Maguire, M., Maines, N., Robinson, E., & Wilson, D. (2006). Not ready to make nice. [Recorded by the Dixie Chicks]. On *Taking the long way.* Columbia Nashville.

Maher, J. (2019, April 17). For the country's most promising teen poets, poetry *is* activism. *Vulture.* Retrieved from https://www.vulture.com/2019/04/the-national-student-poets-programs-teens-fight-for-poetry.html

Muhammmad, G., & Gonzalez, L. (2016). Slam poetry: An artistic resistance toward identity, agency, and activism. *Equity & Excellence in Education, 49*, 440–453. http://dx.doi.org/10.1080/10665684.2106.1126105

Owens, W. (2021). *War poems.* Independent.

Pavlacic, J. M., Buchanan, E. M., Maxwell, N. P., Hopke, T. G., & Schulenberg, S. E. (2019). A meta-analysis of expressive writing on posttraumatic stress, posttraumatic growth, and quality of life. *Review of General Psychology, 23*, 230–250. https://doi.org/10.1177/1089268019831645

Pennebaker, J. W., & Smyth, J. M. (2016). *Opening up by writing it down: How expressive writing improves health and eases emotional pain.* Guilford.

Petroski, W. (2016). Steve King creates uproar questioning contributions of non-white people, *The Des Moines Register.* Retrieved from https://www.desmoinesregister.com/story/news/politics/2016/07/18/steve-king-creates-uproar-salute-to-contributions-of-white-people/87270220/

Phillips, L. T., & Lowrey, B. S. (2018). Herd invisibility: The psychology of racial privilege. *Current Directions in Psychological Science, 27*, 156–162. https://doi.org/10.1177/0963721417753600

Riggs, T. (Ed.). (2015). McCarthyism. In T. Riggs (Ed.), *Gale Encyclopedia of U.S. economic history* (Vol. 2; 2nd ed.). Gale.

Schorn, D. (2006, May 11). Dixie Chicks: Not ready to make nice. *CBS News.* Retrieved from https://www.cbsnews.com/news/dixie-chicks-not-ready-to-make-nice/

Shakur, A. (1987). *Assata: An autobiography.* Lawrence Hill Books.

Travagin, G., Margola, D., & Revenson, T. A. (2015). How effective are expressive writing interventions for adolescents? A meta-analytic review.

Clinical Psychology Review, 36, 42–55.
https://doi.org/10.1016/j.cpr.2015.01.003

van Emmerik, A. A. P., Reijntjes, A., & Kamphuis, J. H. (2013). Writing therapy for posttraumatic stress. *Psychotherapy and Psychosomatics, 82,* 82–88. doi: 10.1159/000343131

Yam, K. (2020, October 15). After Trump's Covid-19 diagnosis, anti-Asian tweets and conspiracy rose 85%: report. *NBC News.* Retrieved from https://www.nbcnews.com/news/asian-america/after-trump-s-covid-19-diagnosis-anti-asian-tweets-conspiracies-n1243441

Poems

Journey of Brilliance
Aliya J'anai

1619! 1619!
Read all about it!
The first Africans were shipped on a journey!

1619! 1619!
350 Africans were taken from their homes and promised a greater destiny!

1619! 1619!
150 Africans died on the ships.

1619.
1619.
Only "20 and odd Negroes" ever made it.

1619...
1619...
The start of 400 years of inequality.

1619...
1619...
The start of 400 years of pure monstrosity.

1619. 1619.
The start of a different kind of resilience!

1619! 1619!
Not the start nor the end of our brilliance!

35,000 B.C.
It was the African people who used the Lebombo Bone
Which is the oldest mathematical artifact ever known!
5000 B.C.
It was the African people who invented the earliest known boat which
they later developed into ships –
So Spanish Colonies wouldn't have even been able to take us across the
ocean if not for the very ships we built...

4000 B.C.
It was the African people who invented the loom for creating textiles for knits.
2630 B.C.
It was the African people who built the first pyramids!
2052 B.C.
It was the African people who created the term "Seba" which is the origin of philosophy.
2000 B.C.
It was the African people who transitioned from the Stone Age and began the Iron Age—they changed history!
Between 350 and 550 A.D.
Antibiotics were being used by the Nubians.
800 A.D.
The first psychiatric hospital was built by the Egyptians.
1100 A.D.
The ventilator was invented in Egypt.
But wait!
It doesn't stop there!
There's more to it!

Through the inventions of African people over centuries, we have:
Math
Calendars,
Maps,
Architecture,
Astronomy,
Navigation,
Meteorology,
And medicine.
1802
Henry Boyd invented the "Boyd Bedstead."
1819
Benjamin Montgomery invented the steamboat propeller.
1821
Thomas Jennings invented dry cleaning.
1878
Lewis Latimer invented the carbon filament for the lightbulb Thomas Edison got credit for.
1892
George T. Sampson invented the clothes dryer.

In the 20th century,
Black people invented the gas furnace,
The automatic gear shift,
Blues and Jazz music,
The traffic light,
Folk and Rock and Roll,
The thermostat,
The pacemaker,
The pencil sharpener,
Peanut butter!
The Super Soaker!!!

And our people did it all in the midst of
Slavery.
Oppression.
Lynchings.
Segregation.
Even in the midst of Redlining.
So, for African people, 1619 may have been the beginning of a new
kind of resilience,
But our people have ALWAYS been on a journey of true brilliance.

The Color of Your Skin
Red Haircrow

The color of your skin
is synonymous with slave,
son or daughter thereof—
servant at the whim of—
'skin under the heel of—.

If you bring this up they say,
'Not us!' 'That's the past!"
Yet their actions reek of it,
and their eyes betray they know
they yet benefit from it.

And you're still
the likely thief,
the probable drunk,
the inevitable drug dealer.
The seducer of husband,
of brother or father,
or threat to chastity
and racial purity.

The color of your skin
is synonymous
with sex, with heat, with threat,
while white virtue is
protected, defended, and
immortalized in song
by the same men
forcing children to submit
or slaughtering you
like animals.

Red is savage.
Brown is bad.
Black is evil.
Labels applied.

White as innocence,
white as goodness,
white as pure when
in actuality it's done
the darkest of deeds with a smile,
and butter unmelted on the tongue.

***

"The Color of Your Skin" was previously published in *Red Ink International Journal,* December 2016. Republished with permission.

"The Color of Your Skin" was previously published in *Geschichte Schrieben-Neue Rundschau,* 2018. Republished with permission.

I Refuse
Nathaniel Granger, Jr.

I refuse
To allow your issues to become my issues
I refuse
To allow your bitterness to make me bitter
The cold glare
The lofty stare
That look that tells me how much you care—
Less about my kind
Less about my mind
Or what I think and what you'd find
If you would let me be
Free me to be me
Allow yourself to give a damn.

I refuse
To allow your degrading thoughts to make me degrade
I refuse
To allow the denigrating messages to make me afraid
Grinding bone
I'm left alone
The Grinch-like smile; I don't belong
To your bourgeois clique
My skin depicts
Something of a nothing that makes you sick
And you don't know why
But refuse to try
To bring yourself to give a damn.

I refuse
To allow your darkness to strangle my light
I refuse
To allow your ugly to extinguish my bright
Isms and schisms
Is what keeps us from giving
To humanity's sake.
Is this really living?
Or a way of survival

That we should be rivals
On the easy road
Toward destruction. Damn!
I refuse.

For Abundance
Veronica Lac

We live our lives of abundance
in the knowledge that we are safe
and sound in our ignorance
of all our privileges
Blinded by the fearmongers
fueling hatred, quenching hope.
Compassion, fatigued
but not helpless, begins to draw strength.

Calling to hearts still open
imploring, pleading
for non-bigotry-contaminated air
to breathe, to restore faith in humanity
To begin to dream once more
for peace, so hard won from sacrifices
Let us not squander or forget
the brave souls upon whose shoulders we stand,
in this land of the free
and home of the brave
Let us give thanks

For abundance, privilege, and lives intact
For family, friends, and community
For all that is dear to us,
whilst not perfect is enough
for us to share
with others who have not,
and those who feel fear
Let us breathe hope
that they find love, acceptance
Let us open our hearts
so that they may have us.

An Innocent Question: "One Check or Two?"
Louis Hoffman

I.
Eyes glisten with love
Over a sparkling ring
Our hands united over the table
Chocolate and milk tones intertwined
Soft voices, a gentle rub
We don't hide our hearts

II.
A perfect night 'til
"Will that be one check or two?"
Our eyes connect with familiar pondering...
An innocent question?
Or intrusive assumption?
Heart rates change
As our thoughts wander
Listening more closely
In the new silence
Other couples aren't offered
Innocent questions.

III.
What was she thinking?
'Surely not them, a couple!'
'She must be a...'
No, I can't write it
I can't think it

IV
A different silence encompasses
Our walk to the car
Still hand in hand
Until I open the door
Tonight, we don't speak it
We have too many times before
One thing clear:
They do not see us

And instead, only "he and she"
They think us a couple
That should not be

V
An innocent question?
Why let it ruin our night?
But to be seen by not being seen
That sends the message
You don't need to say,
"They're polluting the white race"
"That's an abomination" or even
"Their love should not be allowed"
They say it all
In an innocent question

Letter to My Ex
Jennifer O'Neill

You're not that black, you said.
Were you referring to my shade of blackness?
Were you referring to how I act, my hair texture, my education,
Or the way I speak?
Not that black?
What is too black?
Am I too black if my natural hair is kinky?
Am I too black if I use words you don't understand?
Am I too black if I bop my head to Tupac and
Throw my hands in the air and wave them like I just don't care?
I am black.
I know who I am. I don't need a definition.
I am not too much
Or too little.
I'm just enough
Brown sugar with a touch of spice.

Do You Have Any Kids?
Matt Dahl

Because maybe I don't want to tell you about the injectables. The 42 months of trying and failing. The weekly visits to turn my skin into an acupuncturist's pin cushion. The drugs turning my veins into a science experiment. The waiting for the answer, and it's always one line, never two. The sex on a schedule and ultrasounds they do from the inside—did you know that? And the feeder tube; gotta use the feeder tube, because my fallopians aren't shaped quite right. The constant scrutinization of my diet. The worry and self-doubt and abstinence from alcohol. The cupboard shelf of supplements, the ones I hide when you come over so you don't see prenatal vitamins and get excited.

Because the last time we had hope the hope lasted for three months until New Year's Eve. And then the blood and the X-ray and the D&C and now our baby. Yes, we had a baby. Is ashes. And she's in a miniature turquoise urn on the living room shelf.
And instead of hearing oh you can just try again and oh have fun trying, we lie and say no. No kids, not yet.

Because telling you the truth is too messy to do between bites of this goddamn healthy-tasting sandwich. I guess that's why I just tell you no.

Evolve
Joy L. S. Hoffman

It is convenient to call me your Asian friend,
Your Asian family member,
The child you saved.
But I am not your justification.

Stop telling your friends about me,
How you don't see my skin,
My eyes, my hair,
My life.
I am not your color blindness.

When I speak loudly,
Assertively,
Confidently,
Your discomfort and anger prove
That I am not your model minority.

You stare,
Glare,
And act like I am your worst nightmare,
But you still won't wear your mask.
I am not a virus.

You fear me out of ignorance,
generational hate,
and lies your teachers told you.
I am not that history lesson.

You value what you can exotify,
And dream of control and pleasure.
You think it's a compliment.
I am not your fetishization.

You ask me where I'm from
And won't accept my answer
Until it fits your assumptions
I am not your ignorance.

You recruit me because I'm brown,
Ask for impossible outcomes,
Then blame me for your insidious culture.
I am not your scapegoat.

You pit me against my siblings
Black and brown,
And embolden a zero-sum game.
I am not your wedge.

I AM the strength of my ancestors,
The joy of community,
The power of solidarity,
The healing in my soul,
And compassion of my heart.

After the grief,
The fear,
The rage,
And exhaustion,
I am always,
Quite surprisingly,
Hopeful.

The Robbery of Rosalind Franklin*
Carol Barrett

for Anne Sayre

You tell us lost facts
are not always replaceable:
biography too cruel

a word for a life
spiraling into oblivion.
Watson? A very fine art

to be persuasive so briefly,
post-mortem, at that.
You broke the phantom

spectacles his ego invented,
led us to the plain light
that was hers, sketching

a landscape in perspective
at the age of eight,
the carpenter's bench

for fine dovetail
and miter. What she touched
she adorned. In crystallography,

in graphite, in carbons,
her goal: illuminate
elusive structure.

She followed a line
of prophets: Isaiah
planted selective seeds.

Mendel mixed the smooth-skinned
and the wrinkled. His peas
have fourteen chromosomes.

Horses, 64. (Did Watson
get more than his share?)
In a widow's room, bookshelves

crowned with statuary
to fit the ceiling, Rosalind
bartered lessons in French

conjugations and cooking.
Frame and beauty, her guides.
Sugar rationed, she longed

for sticky cakes, not
the Irish pub in the Strand
where they primed

her assistant for the curled
threads of her work. Watson claims
she came from behind

the lab bench to assault him.
He was the assailant, attributing
the discovery he needed

he would use—the location
of the sugar-phosphate
backbone of the molecule

on the *outside* looking in,
as Rosalind must, outside,
look in—to the outpourings

of a misguided feminist.
She was robbed. The rest
of her life she dismantled

viruses in an old house
bombed in the war, afterward
cobbled together. Her beakers

and pots caught the drips,
room on the fifth floor,
the last stairs twisted

against the wall. She refused
cancer's tourniquet, needling
deadly polio in the cellar.

Of Watson's stealth Rosalind
was innocent, never asked,
nor guessed, never was told.

Watson's one regret:
she didn't build better models.
He liked a noisy burial.

The moral of his story:
winner take all. Of yours:
let us unsilence her life.

* Rosalind Franklin discovered the helical structure of DNA. Working without the support enjoyed by her male colleagues, and contributing to the uncovering of the genetic code, she died before Watson, who with cohort Crick received the Nobel prize for the work, published *The Double Helix*, describing a woman he called "Rosy" with disdain and deceit. To correct the record, Anne Sayre wrote *Rosalind Franklin and DNA*.

***

"The Robbery of Rosalind Franklin" was previously published in *The Women's Review of Books*, 1990, Volume VII(5), p. 14. Republished with permission from *The Women's Review of Books*.

"The Robbery of Rosalind Franklin" was previously published in *Spectral Lines: Poems about Scientists* (2019, Alternating Current Press). Republished with permission.

Complicated
J. Thomas Brown

When you're ambitious and decide to play,
Life's a scramble every day
You slide your pawns past gated borders
To play the big game in foreign quarters

Politicians fill your mind
And important people with social ties
They're overrated, selfish, and unkind
And you must stay a jump ahead
Or they will have their way instead
Now the game gets complicated

Throughout the globe in every quarter
Flows the sludge of the New World Order,
Through pipelines of necrotic veins
Beneath the oceans to foreign shores
To surface in tumult and costly wars
It's very complicated

You sold your soul to Beelzebub
To join the New World social club
Enjoyed the veneration of the masses
Have been adored by all the classes

Yours is the grip and crush of power
Toppling giants like World Trade Towers
But there won't ever be enough
Of the narcotic drug of complicated stuff

You set them flaming, took them down
With precision to the ground
The finest hour of Beelzebub
So obfuscated, so deeply, very complicated

Life seems simple in its way
We do the same things everyday
And growing old we never doubt

We've come to know what it's about
Then your reasoning shall be ablated
As past mistakes are contemplated,
When it's too late to have regret
You were deeply, so completely, complicated

***

"Complicated" was previously published in *Mooncalf* by J. Thomas Brown (2020, Fenghuang Publishing). Republished with permission.

Becoming Formless:
Opening Doors We Didn't Know Existed
Vanessa Sinclair

With the establishment
of the patriarchy
comes the delineation of gender.
What makes a man?
And
what makes a woman?
The patriarchy
establishes an entire system of culture
created to perpetuate itself.
It continually enforces and reinforces
its own system, which it created.

Patriarchy defines
masculine characteristics
in positive terms
while the
feminine is negative.
Patriarchy also establishes and enforces the binary,
of the opposition
masculine–feminine
in the unconscious.

The subject is inserted into he/r
sexual nature,
sexuality preceding the *I*.
Attempts to grasp onto an identity
can be seen as
one grappling
with sexuality,
with one's intrinsic sexual nature,
attempting to categorize
it,
restrict it,
contain it,

and give it a limit

in an effort to control it.

established in the original argument
and is continually operated and
reinforced by the system it created.
The question now is what happens
when such a patriarchal system begins to be put into question.
When its
structure of gender and prescribed role patterns
begins to crumble.

Historically, during times of instability
when the patriarchal structure was
put into question
there was merely an exchange
of one primal father for
another.
Take down a king and replace him with another king.
The system
formless void
in which our periodic table of elements
as well as the human form
was created.

As
humans
we are predestined to regimen.
There is routine and there is deviation.
If we look at
the cut up technique
designed by Brion Gysin
we can see a connection
between routine and
the room,
with a first come first serve policy each morning.
This disrupted attachment to
material possessions,
personal space,
privacy,
separation between self and others.
When

that takes down the previous system
ends up being structurally the same
underneath.
One revolution
replaces another
and then becomes the ruler.

Such choral techniques
also have a separating or discriminating
effect,
as in threshing,
an image that Plato employs in his
Love,
warmth,
exploration,
creating memories in me and so many others.
I'm so honored to
have met you.
Your passing makes no sense.
Death seldom does.
Your leaving us so soon will
have to be a motivation,
an incentive to value life
even more.
And not waste even a moment
of it.

In the current situation, hopefully,
the system is being deconstructed and
there is a real fight against maintaining the status quo.
Heart to heart and soul to soul,
we can and will carry on
doing what we do.
Art to art and role
to role,
we will keep your memory alive,
loving you
for who you were,
still are,
and always
will be.

"It was definitely inspired by alchemy and the idea of the
hermaphrodite.
In folklore, the
original human or the original virus.
And also an angelic representation of humans.
That
image fascinated us
because this was a way of being that was fruitful in every possible
way:
an artist's muse.
The hermaphrodite is a symbol of creative potential."
'The daughter of Babylon is like a threshing floor.
It is time to
thresh her:
yet a little while
and the time of her harvest will
come.

deviation.
According to Brion Gysin and William S. Burroughs
the cut up technique is a
juxtaposition of language
cutting up written texts
to form new text
creating third mind.
Looking
at deviation
we can see that it is essentially a physical cut up
that can be done at will
or by the
unconscious mind
at any moment.
Chaos is third mind.
Third mind is deviation,
therefore
becoming formless
in the state of being
through
both
conscious and the unconscious.

Morose Music
Keith Wallace

The music played,
but I felt no desire to dance,
and prance, or move my feet.
I needed to digest B flats, and D sharps and F minors,
with no buds, no taste,
just saliva dribbling black snowflakes,
under my tongue.

I heard angry music stutter,
sprinkling bitter bullets
that turned gray, then blue, then green with eyes of anger.
They tumbled over kisses and flags and 9mm guns,
that morphed into melodies of hate.
Everything you see or hear,
don't just embrace it, or even disdain it,
but measure it with love.

Then Confederate flags, Swastikas, and banners of Racism,
will lose their potency.
They will transform into Rum and Raisin ice cream.
Crave it, eat it, crunch it,
then you'll hear music,
E flats, G sharps, and A sharp majors,
dissolving into pink snowflakes under your tongue.

Chicago Sonnet #4

D. A. Hosek

Perhaps he thought the first rock was a joke
Just a playful reminder of the line between
Black and white, north and south; just stay
On your side of that invisible boundary.

But water holds no lines, knows no divisions
And why couldn't he belong at one beach
As much as any other? A rock to the head
Is the answer he receives; water fills his lungs.

The stoner walks free, the injustice obvious
And the (Black) bystanders protest, only
To see one of their number hustled to jail.
Is it any wonder that this was not the End?

Rocks on the beach became rocks in the streets
And a hundred years later the wound still bleeds.

"What If Justice Was Fair?"
Laura Wright

They say just get over it but the question
remains how when everyday another life
hangs in the balance and the world hears silence.

When black culture mobilizes its mutiny the outcries
begin to yell out kill them all better yet soon as the
tables turn and you see fit to benefit it's labeled as
an assault on our democracy and even still you're set free.

What about those who look like me after all you did
say our democracy or is that just the hypocrisy in each
and every one of you the chosen few that get to choose
all the rules while we sit an' play foolish fools.

Again, I ask you who made up this game where the
rules simply never change and the outcome stays
exactly the same built on a constitution that fails
to give all of my people their restitution.

Living in a world with no peace watching my brothers,
and sisters, die in the streets how can they compete if
the competition is a ghost who died before they were
born but your judges uphold their laws without cause.

A race still fighting to be equal in a world that claims
liberty and justice for all choking back tears every time
we saw an applaud or even a knee in protest during
the national anthem especially knowing you hated them.

Remember, we fought those same wars right beside
you when you needed us we were your brothers and
sisters in arms until we got discharged then we became
the number two enemy of the state the ones you all hate.

Now before you go making excuses ask yourself what's
the use the truth has been on display for months without
delay Netflix made a movie even twisted it their own way.

If someone told you today Black Lives Matter would you
agree, or would your reply be Blue Lives Matter if that's
the case did it matter when your people stormed the Capital
where is the outcry was his life not worthy it should be if any
of you truly cared about What If Justice Was Fair.

These Eyes That Can No Longer Weep
Esther Muthoni Wafula

Based on events during the genocide in Rwanda

These eyes that can no longer weep
These are a child's eyes
Intently studying each lifeless face
From end to end
Of the mass grave
Where mother, father and friend
Where the nation lies still
In painful unjustifiable death
These eyes helplessly close
To let heartrending scenes
Pass unseen

But,
They leave behind sounds
Footfalls of running soldiers
Bullets swiftly shattering
They leave behind memories
The face of a friend turned foe
Machetes in merciless murder
Helpless groans of a sister, a brother
In the throes of death.

These eyes that could no longer weep
These are a child's eyes
In which tears suddenly rise
Lingering
Surprised
Unbelieving
That the sun still shines
Across the sky indifferent
That the wind still whistles
As it used to
Before the war
Before death came
Doesn't the sun see this misery

Doesn't the wind hear this wailing
Doesn't the world feel this pain?

Genocide
Louis Hoffman

"Old Navy supports the GENOCIDE of the White race!"
~ Response on Twitter to Old Navy featuring a mixed-race family

I.

The wall melted into the floor
dripping names as if blood
unable to stand, I
sat, stunned into stillness
the hand on mine gripped tight
as we gulped tears
mourning Rwanda,
a country we did not know

II.

Katrina flooded our TV screen
and swept us away.
"They all look just like me"
words that haunt like an angry ghost
as tears streamed on ebony

The names never stop:
Trayvon Martin
Tamir Rice
Michael Brown
Sandra Bland
Freddie Gray
Eric Garner
George Floyd...
Names blurred together
as tears form trails of
red mixed with black

III.

In anger they cry out:
"#WhiteGenocide"
claiming "forced integration"
as the weapon

Blonde hair, blue eyes
loving a beautiful black woman
= genocide

Mocha children
crying at the unjust world

Love,
they say,
is genocide

III.

They turned the lights off
in fear
The familiar road now bumpy
They step out
on this content so
colonized that it lives on
without the original oppressor:
Bodies everywhere
roads flowing with blood

The world looks on
soldiers are told not to act
while politicians debate definitions
no matter how deep blood
soaks into this land
there is no oil
there is no gold
and the world looks on

This Poem Was Brought to You By the Letter "P"

Jennifer K. Yancey

Pardon this interruption
Good evening, Mr. and Mrs. America
And all the ships at sea ~
Newsflash:
Our planet is in peril!
Perplexed?
Ponder living in a
Perpetual state of
Panic
Previewed as prey
By persons who painstakingly pursued
You
As their favorite pastime
To them it's a constant
State of play
A simply puerile state of mind.

Plainly put
Their persistence
Pushes them to be persuaded
By their perverted
Sense of pride
Thus your pigmentation,
A symbol of perfection,
Is in direct violation
Of Articles w, h, i, t and e.

While pelted by the media's
Projectile vomiting
Promoting the practice of
Character assassination,
Pride pleads for them to
Pull you apart
And peer into your soul
That attempted to escape
From your fetid corpse
They left hemorrhaging in the streets.

Punished disproportionately
In the classroom
Trauma in the pre-K
Palpitations riddle the hearts
Of chocolate cherubs
Portrayed as pint-sized
Felons-in-waiting
Pursuant to the school-to-prison
Pipeline ~
So you see
All is going according to plan.

Yesterday was the time
To start practicing your
Huey P.
Black Panther
Pistol grip.
Today is NOT the day
To lose your religion
But to start planning
Insurrection and revolt
And purge patriarchy
Like the pussies
You were plucked from
At birth.

The time has passed
For the peacemaker
We don't seek reconciliation
With those who purloined
Our persons and property ~
Where is your passion?
Did you use it all up for the
Pledge?

Well make a promise to your own
Self
That you will not go quietly
Into the night
Paralyzed into inaction, by fear
Instead,

Quicken your pace
Pass me the mobile so we can record the
Furious styles of a
Millennium revolution
Pulsating at a fevered pitch …
Then, pause, for effect.

Brightest Smile
Nathaniel Granger, Jr.

At the red light
On the off ramp
I-25 and Uinta
Running late
I stop

On the left
Squatting
His leathered skin,
Maroon
And weathered by struggle

His gaze fixed
On nothing
In the weed-strewn gravel
Not future, not hope,
Nothing.

Above head
Attached to splintered wood
The inscription
"Homeless Vet"
Proved not his humanity

Suspect, U.S. Army vet
Gave life for the rights
And freedoms of the passersby
Who wish him dead
Wish he'd leave

At best,
A veteran of survival
An old soldier
Of the streets, bridges,
Viaducts and boxcars

My advent was hardly noticed
Shadow blurred by fleeting cloud
I give the backpack from my trunk
Necessities for war
He looks up

Weary eyes fill with glee
Deepened crow's feet etch their corners
Bottomless dimples puncture cheeks
Teeth rotted, jagged, missing
All tobacco-tatted with time

The light turns green
I slowly drive off
Relishing the gift
A grateful heart
The brightest smile.

Esther Counsels the Wife of a Confederate General
Carol Barrett

When he's gone, you conjure his breath
beside you in the dark, like moss
at the wellhouse where Gramps
taught you dominoes, the black and white
lined up and falling together,
where you drank lemonade
with cousins from Willow Creek.

I know. I do my own conjuring.
After the wedding feast, I tasted the tart
knowledge of chicory on his tongue,
so unlike the woolly incense
they steeped me in, soft smoke
circling long wraps at the waist,
mixing with my maidenhair.
After the wedding dance, they washed
your petticoats clean of the dark polish
that brightened his boots.

You recall such things, alone
on the path, flowers either side of the stone.
The blue. The gray. Honeysuckle climbs
the brush, both sides of the road,
twining its lush stranglehold.
Who can say what your roots oblige?
They did not name God in my story.
They name God both sides of yours.

Tonight in dreams you will watch
those boots kick bayonets in trenches,
rolls of sweet hay barricading the barn,
chickens flapping with crippled wings.
When the new light saunters up the road
like a foolhardy friend, you go out
to still them, but all the eggs

are broken, each fresh sun
spilled in a yard of puddled yolks.

I had such dreams, lambs bleating
in the countryside, stone walls overturned.
We hesitate for the years, your quilts
and sunbonnets, my palms of olive,
my train of feathered gold.
I passed as a Persian bride. You passed
as pure strain, no ants in the sugar.

Tomorrow at your mirror when the day
goes dim, sparrows burrow in to dusk,
touch the fine hair at your temples
that wants to curl, no matter the long
straight strokes, your nanny's bristle brush
trying to tame its sweet dark secret.

Then lift a child to your face, any child
with damp, warm brow. Ask yourself:
Could I be mother to more than mine,
sister even to a race of angels,
sleek black Seraphim
streaming over the relentless war,
the bleeding, all one color in the spill?

You choose, as I chose.
Under cover of dark you will saddle your dead
brother's stallion and ride to camp,
the miles snapping like twigs
in the smell of muskets.
You will make your way in to his chambers.
You will count on this: only some mossy affection
when your hair was tousled and wet.

How do you tell your man he is wrong?
You weigh all the costs like flour,
turnips and chard trampled under hooves,
that child you once were kneeling beside the well
where the bucket now comes up crimson.

Finally, you ask what your own life
bears, place it in the balance.

***

"Esther Counsels the Wife of a Confederate General" was previously published in *The Unauthorized Book of Esther: New Poems and Commentary on Revisionist Biblical Literature* by Carol Barrett (1998; Doctoral Dissertation, Union Institute and University, Cincinnati, OH).

"Esther Counsels the Wife of a Confederate General" was previously published in *Bridges* (2000). Republished with permission from *Bridges*.

"Esther Counsels the Wife of a Confederate General" was previously published in *Solum Journal* (2020). Republished with permission from *Solum Journal.*

"Esther Counsels the Wife of a Confederate General" was previously published in *For a Better World 2021* (2021). Republished with permission.

Robber Baron
J. Thomas Brown

Of all the things I'd like to be
A robber baron's the life for me
I'd have piles of money and shuffle it about
Put some in, take some out
Of dozens of corporations, either inactive or dissolved
In order to hide it when taxes are involved

I'd spend like a sailor and brag quite a bit
Of who I know and on whom I'd shit
I'd sue my neighbors and laugh when they squeal
Then turn around and offer a deal;
They must change their shrubbery and build a new fence
If you had any brains, you'd know that makes sense

When I'm a robber baron, how objective I'd be
Being selfish is the way to build the economy
The wealth flows down with each mad money caper
And before you know it, your name is written
On every skyscraper

I'm an Ayn Randist and know what I'm doing
Forget the losers and suckers I'm screwing
I have twenty-one children and seven ex-wives
They deserve the best for the rest of their lives
And though Jaguars and Mercedes are nice
I'll buy each a Ferrari without asking the price

Don't get me wrong, I'm not a bad fellow
When I grow old, I'm going to mellow
I promise to try to give it away
To hedge my bets for judgment day
Or pay someone else to write a nice book
About how I am good, and not just a crook

***

"Robber Barron" was previously published in *Mooncalf* by J. Thomas Brown (2020, Fenghuang Publishing). Republished with permission.

No Trespassing
Jyl Anais

One day, I'll walk
without invitations for rides
shouted by men in
pickup trucks
driving in the opposite direction.
Straight to Hell,
that is.

And wait for a bus
without an incessant flow of questions
regarding my marital status
whether I've been incarcerated
or not, as though that
would explain why
I'm not married
yet
and whether I'm looking for a boyfriend
and why not,
whether I'll take their phone numbers
to call when I'm ready
for one.
Constant harassment
imbeds itself
in me.

I think I'll tattoo
"No Trespassing"
across my chest
after all,
and walk with
a pit bull named "Happy"
my body between
sandwich boards that read,
like the sign
in Isabel's bedroom did,

No hunting
or fishing, here.

***

"No Trespassing" was previously published in *The Urban Howl* (2016). Republished with permission.

"No Trespassing" was previously published in *Nixes Mate Review* (2019). Republished with permission.

"No Trespassing" was previously published in *Soft Out Spoken* by Jyl Anais (2019, Sin Miedo Press). Republished with permission.

El Chucho
Jim Keller

A sound outside
El Chucho barks
Carlos roused from sleep
opens the door to the ICE men
several and large
El Chucho barks again and growls
But Carlos shakes his finger
and points to his bed
He goes reluctantly
continuing to growl and
stare at the men now in his house
speaking a strange,
harsh tongue
The family all awake
begin gathering their things
into black garbage bags
Maria helping the children

At last a man opens the door
Carlito and Angelina
bawling, hug their Chucho
Outside El Chucho tries to follow
But Carlos says No!
And points to the back yard
El Chucho goes only to the side of the house
and watches his family taken away
in the dark vans

Now El Chucho sleeps under his car
against a wheel that blocks
the wind and the snow
Food left by Carlito and Angelina
is gone
as is the water
He is cold, hungry and very thirsty
El Chucho cries
But no one hears or cares

***

American Dream On
Sean Murphy

Your America
is not Me.
Your History
is not My story.

When your head's buried
in cloudy contentment:
I come to life.

I don't punch any clock,
I ain't no nine-to-five.
So what you see isn't
always what you'll get.
But bet that what you get's
always what you paid for.

Dancing to music
you don't hear
(You can't).

Seeing God/
Being God.
I got you covered.

It's a war I never started.
But one I'll always need.

This land is your land,
but when you buy
you belong to me.

What goes around never comes around,
but what goes up always comes down.
So you'll come see me. Again.

A hard road ahead like a marked vein.

And each day's a new wave
crashing on this concrete shore.
Like a rusted syringe.

The Ballad of Sandra Bland
Katherine Edgren

Heading to a job at Prairie View
she landed in the County Jail.
If she'd been white, she'd be alive,
instead of under the coffin nail.

A feisty, young black activist—
a firebrand, you understand—
if it's meekness that you seek
turn away from Sandra Bland.

College degree—summer counselor—
Volunteer —in a band—
a brilliant job starting soon:
the criminal past of Sandra Bland.

Driving through Waller County
she met her nemesis.
Just once she didn't signal,
this: the awful genesis.

On her way and full of life
failure to show a change in lane
warped into a capital offense
after a heated exchange

with Brian Encinia, Texas Cop,
whose version of respect—
what he said that he most wanted—
extinguishing her cigarette.

Exit the car he ordered,
taser in his hand.
His eyes grew wide: *I'll light you up!*
Who's your Master, Sandra Bland?

A taser delivers compliance
using fiery electroshock

subduing what's highly dangerous:
unneeded in a traffic stop.

He tossed her to the dirty ground,
the way to command respect.
He turned into a two-bit tyrant,
his knee upon her neck.

She was a wily fish
wriggling on the handcuff-hook.
In netting this scrappy specimen,
he threw away the book.

And he arrested her.
Pulled over for a traffic violation.
On her way, full of life—
soon: a wrongful death investigation.

They took her to a Texas jail.
Twenty-eight, and far from home.
Why oh why she asked again?
They tossed her in a cell, alone.

*How did failure to signal
turn into all of this?*
We failed you, Sandra Bland
in this nightmare of madness.

At 9 am the jailer found her
hanging in her cell,
hanging from a garbage bag.
She'd known some kind of hell.

Those who knew her cried *foul play.*
The jailors named it suicide.
In one upbeat about her job,
her friends suspected homicide.

A soldier and a warrior in the
BLM campaign; never lazy.

Depression, THC in her blood—
they tried to call her crazy.

Dash cam tapes showed up: edited.
The truth remains a mystery.
The jail failed a suicide watch.
We hold her now in memory.

The family was paid a settlement.
Injustice *had* stalked the land.
The cop was fired, taser retired.
Black Lives Matter, Sandra Bland.

Now all across this murderous land,
as people roam the street,
we sing an elegy for Sandra Bland.
Without justice, there is no peace.

***

"The Ballad of Sandra Bland" was previously published in *The Grain Beneath the Gloss* by Katherine Edgren (Finishing Line Press, 2017). Republished with permission.

Don't Swallow

J. Thomas Brown

the foods we eat today
are full of toxic spray
the genes from which they sprung
are spliced with dungbeetle bacterium
it's really very sad,
but they can drive you MAD

neuro-toxins cause alarm,
aspartame will send you to the funny farm
you'll flip your lid, you'll go insane
as your synapses burst into flame
nothing's ever scarier
when they slip through your brain barrier

if your John Thomas
lacks in promise
Viagra is for you
after three or four hours
she'll send you flowers
and shout a hurrah or two

but should her desire
be under the wire
there's something for her too
with just one pill
she'll feel a new thrill
and keep going the whole night through

never mind you go blind,
or suffer a stroke,
have headaches, seizures, or choke
while you're still able,
read the label
it's a sexistential joke

it's all for the better,
they know what's best

they just don't have time to run a test
it's really very sad
there's nothing you can do,
but don't swallow if it's FDA approved

***

"Don't Swallow" was previously published in *Mooncalf* by J. Thomas Brown
(2020, Fenghuang Publishing). Republished with permission.

Chicago Sonnet #27
D. A. Hosek

Where once dismal towers loomed over
the streets, bright townhomes clump like dandelions.
Dominick's on Division was just another
premonitory sign of changing times.

Gone are the liquor store, gone are the young
men on the corners slinging to stopped cars,
gone are the children who tried to have fun,
in lots pocked with glass shards, who carried their scars

deep in the shadow of a childhood lost
in Mother Cabrini's occluded light.
Now they're dispersed: mere trash thoughtlessly tossed
away. Just more rubbish of urban blight.

These newly sanitized, clean and empty ways
bear no traces of dangerous olden days.

A Long-Standing War
Kelsey Smith

We're a nation of neighbors,
That are strangers,
And we don't even realize
The inherent danger.
Cut like a razor,
A nation in two,
Black against blue.
You say we're self-righteous,
But we're not riotous.
Come and fight with us.
Come say your words.
Be heard.
Yeah, I'm scared of violence,
But even more terrified by my silence.
I can't sit still while my friends are being murdered,
And the cops are acquitted
Not even perjured.
What's the precursor for change?
The whole damn system is deranged.
Time to completely rearrange ourselves.
Get in formation,
Civilian soldiers.
There's a war raging on.
King capitalism is holding strong.
Stop acting like nothing's wrong.
Open your eyes and see
My hand is reaching for you.
We need you to help us move.
We've all got something to prove.
And we've all got something to lose.
Some more than others,
So come on dude,
Protect your brothers
Mothers without children,
Weeping in the streets
And still we don't hear a single peep from you?
You think you're safe if you stay quiet,

But violence is a hungry beast,
And after he's feasted on our last bit of flesh
He'll move on to you.
And while you were grazing from your silver spoon,
We were brought to your end too soon.
So now you're alone in an empty room.
And now you're the system's victim.
You've provided your own prison
Because you didn't listen.
And there's no one left to set you free.
You shouldn't have abandoned me.
Because when you did,
You swallowed your own key.

Inhale. Hold.
Nance Reynolds

I. Mississippi Air 1958

Droplets of moisture float in the breeze this afternoon
Usual and ordinary here.
Beads of water so tiny they become invisible
Swallowed up day and night,
by symmetrical needles of bald cypress,
stately polished leaves of southern magnolia ...
clusters of crape myrtle.

A breeze moves, perhaps soft and soothing—in some moments ...
But not ours.
Drifts between layers of inspiration and expiration.
in our moment soft is suspended.
and cannot be persuaded to return.

Tidily tucked under a large wooden rocking chair
    is a very young girl in yellow shorts, calico top and canvas sneakers.
Imagining beyond this narrow porch—a real story reveals, uninvited.
she is small enough to fit in secretive places just like a mouse.
Watching.
Fear permeates the air suddenly—
with great precision skeletal muscles freeze in place
vision narrows like a fox for deeper watching.
White girl.

For in this moment the wolf pack approaches
    randomly they move from one street corner, kitty-corner.
Shaped like men these wolves gather and form—as if by magic.
True wolves alpha, beta, epsilon, zeta, mu and chi—rank for survival
keep purposeful rhythm with nature.

These are men—another species.
Vastly distant from the wolf....in some ways.
These men leashed by illusion of superiority,
Noses so low they could kiss the unforgiving concrete, warming
asphalt,

or the grass—so green.
Hard breezes over hard Mississippi ground.
Following you.

Your matching hat, impeccable suit..
bow tie for perfect accompaniment.
Adorning a distinguished tall and long stride.
a stride that defines a courteous man crossing an innocent street.
Inhale.
Your matching hat has toppled....
Hold.
Black man.

With swift agility and calm you duck low for retrieval,
Keeping focus
Amidst threat declaring itself, infused with palpable aggression
As silently the pack howls.

Wincing pain sweeps through the girl in yellow shorts, calico top and
canvas sneakers beneath the rocking chair.
Pain reaches to the deepest center point of bones—harrowing,
    as your black hat topples.
Grace. Pleading.
Inhale. Don't run.

Is this command heard from within?
Child eyes long to scream "*Run, Run!*"
Wolf pack continues to approach....
heart muscles drum violently within,
Enduring beyond time.
Overcome by a primal urge to rear back stand up.
Tall. Upright. Focused.
dislodge the predators from your back,
meeting hard Mississippi ground. Hard.

The heart harnesses immense force in reply—one with dreams.
Dreams of survival.
Dreams of many colors.
Dreams to protect delicate chambers within.
Dreams of breaking the spell.

The heart
Yours. Walking across the innocent street
Mine. Tucked tightly under the gray rocking chair,
small girl trembles, pleading for Grace,
... just like a beggar with a bowl.

Inhale. Hold.

II. **Florida Air   2012**

Moonlit winter evening.
Stillness poised in every breath,
Usual and ordinary here.
Beads of water so tiny they become invisible,
symmetrical needles of bald cypress,
stately polished leaves of southern magnolia...
clusters of crape myrtle,
Drinking in sustenance, whispering tonight.

Megascops asio Eastern screech owl, here now.
Feather and branch pair creating supreme camouflage.
small enough to fit in secretive places
Far far above the hard Florida ground.
Watching.
a condition of stillness drapes this night as you enter and as you leave.

Young man walks with head covered
providing protection? perhaps from within or without—
We don't know.
In another small second a car and a man confront
Threat has declared itself loudly.
    a craving for capture permeates the air as pursuit is joined by
chase,
told to halt "not to follow," but you disobey....
Nose so low, it could kiss the unforgiving concrete, warm asphalt
    or grass—so green.
Hard stillness over hard Florida ground.
Following you.

 Threat is declared authority, ultimatum pronounced.
Focus becomes untouchable, invisible like beads of water in the air.

"Don't Run" "Don't Fight"
Inhale.
For you have become prey.
For you cannot stand your ground.
For you, the color of your skin dictates every move.
Hold.
black man.

Screechless owl—the only one watching
    the young man walking. walking along.
just walking.... on a moonlit Florida night.

III. **With Liberty and Justice for All**

Awaiting birth.
Oh, such a long and excruciating labor.
Centuries turn and words echo endlessly
        through our dark and cavernous history.
Trickster words "liberty and justice for all"... changing shape like the
sky.
Breathless—and asking again and again
Where are you?

Upper New York Bay suspends the symbolic island—rooted.
 Our goddess of liberty promises us freedom and equality for all.
Is this story in our imagination?
        searching the shoreline desperately as waters ebb and flow
Real
Ideal
Real
Ideal.
A flipping coin.
"Liberty and justice for all"—for who ?
 white skinned people with plenty can depend--
others await hazard.

Justice bobs in the New York Bay—
        up and down, unsteady as she goes.
Choppy waters obscure promises formed with words without shape.
            due process of the law
            verdicts concluded with bias built on racist foundation

legislation doomed toward inequality from initial mark of pen
to paper.
United States of America moving in stormy seas with fatal
consequence...

 Yet we seek you... Justice.
Trembling hearts and troubled minds endure
without interruption we move—
As small as a mouse, as keen as an owl
        with certainty—as infinite as the starry sky.

In our quest toward you

Exhale.

Dying in the Sun
Gina Belton

Brown skin, Red skin, hangs
Like fruit drying in the sun
Is this the right way?

What is that? In the tree?
Like fruit drying in the sun?
Brown skin, Red skin hangs

Rapists, drug dealers
Bad hombres, "yeah, we remember you"
Your brown skin, red skin

Like fruit, hanging and
Dying in the sun
And does anyone...

...remember Sandra Bland,
Her brown skin hanging alone?
No place in the sun.

Home Grown
Bernardine (Dine) Watson

There is a whisper on the wind
a soft yet chilling, fearsome, moan
that clutches at the land
from east to west to north
and hovers low above the south
the bible belt
where holy words sit ever reverent
on the lips of child and man.
So listen now and know the piteous plaint
that rises from this place
and promises
no peace no rest
'til penitence is made.

As history will tell
it was a few short scores ago
when grisly terror reigned across this land.
No state was spared
this sin performed as bloody sport.
A people hunted by the rabid mob
a heinous hell hound on their trail.
No rule of law
no moral code
just past-time played in light of day
in the shadow of the courthouse door.

Rope chain knife tree
match fire kerosene.
The scent of negro barbeque.
A carnival to show the young
an outing for the ladies and the finest gents.

Hey mister, want a souvenir?
An eye, a heart, an ear
a piece of bone or flesh
still burning from the scorching flame?

A bold and public spectacle
a bestial show
lest anyone forget
this is the way we do them here.

Four thousand citizens and likely more
no sanctuary in their land
no justice for their terrible loss
no monument where their bodies hung
just a wailing whisper on the wind
to tell the tale
to warn us of the legacy we bear
the terror here across this land
that festers still
no state is spared.

This is the strange and bitter stain
that we must fight, degrade, destroy
and not just in some foreign place
but here
where penitence is due
or there will be
no peace no rest
no rest no peace
for anyone.

Move Along Now
Melinda Rose

Park bench empty
Shelter full
Clouds fill the sky.
Crumbs in my pocket for the gull.

Guess it'll rain
What do we care?
Brisk winds shift
Walkway is bare.

Move along now, I'm told.
Even the gull has flown.
It's drizzlin' and rainin', girl.
You ought not to be out here alone.

Let's Make a New Sign of the Times
Nancy Devine

What if you had
to be a cartographer,
make bathroom maps
of your town,
determine empty or
full?

Maybe a teacher
at your old school,
let you slip
into her office,
use the private stall there.
Still wouldn't your gut
always be in
some untenable threshold?

Legends and borders,
rivers and roads...
what if you had
to travel such distances
just to go?

What if you had
to be a special envoy,
plead for detente
in shopping malls
or ice cream shops,
never able to relax, yourself?

Maybe a small woman
with a big scoop
gave you gelato
and the time you needed
to taste it. Maybe a clerk
didn't question your choice of
accessories...the dangling bracelet
or the gaudy bola or the cummerbund,

the delicate ruching at your waist.

And you could be
where you are
as others beside you did the same
What if I implore you?
What if?
How might we become
if given the room?

The United States of America
Joseph Ellison Brockway

The mahogany of the wood of the four walls of my house,
the house that protects me from storms,
shelters me.

The ochre seed coat of the almond that nourishes my body,
oil that moisturizes my skin,
milk that hydrates me.

The black of the coal that warms me in the dead of winter,
the white of the snow that melts to revive the Earth's trees,
the brown of those trees that shade me from the summer sun,
the brown trees that become paper,
the paper of our laws.

The tan of the sturdy oak of the wooden ties that steady the rails,
the tan of the Chinese who labored on the railroad that united
the two halves of our country.

The copper of tools, of coins, of the skin of Native Americans,
life-sustaining copper in every human body,
the copper of Lady Liberty.

Harriet Tubman, Martin Luther King, Jr., Barack Obama . . .
Abraham Lincoln, Harvey Milk, Gloria Steinem . . .
María Latigo de Hernández, Luis Muñoz Marín, César Chávez . . .
Nellie Wong, George Takei, Kamakahukilani . . .
Squanto, Sacagawea, Sitting Bull . . .

The beautiful shades of this nation.

Don't Want to Write No Poem
Portia Rawles

Don't wanna write no poem.

Don't wanna waste time with flowery words and metaphorical statements.

Don't wanna write no poem.

Too many ancestors still screaming from their graves.

Too many bodies hidden by haze of burning crosses, burning churches.

Don't wanna write no poem.

Fight, maybe?

I Charge Thee
Jennifer K. Yancey

I charge thee
With refusing to teach me my history
I attended your institutions just for the transcript; experience helped
   me obtain my
Education
I charge thee
With your playing the role of God
Using His Word to justify your maltreatment of fellow members of the
   human race
Determining we are less than
That we are only a *fraction* of a man
I charge thee
With not-so-subtle racism
We can't park a car, work out in a gym, or sit in a Starbucks without
   your scrutiny, your suspicion, your resentment over our presence
I charge thee
With simply not leaving me be
Keep following me around in your establishments, we'll shut the b---h
   down
You don't deserve our dollars
I charge thee
With willful stupidity
The facts are in front of you, but you cling to the stereotype
You've already convicted me in the court of public opinion
Based on the implicit bias already ingrained in your psyche
I charge thee
With making me feel unsafe, unwelcome and unwanted in my own
   country
I don't know if my uniform ever really protected me
If I were still serving – *definitely* not
I charge thee
With the objectification of the Black Woman and demonization of the
   Black Man
Your fragility has gotten us Women fired, marginalized, brutalized
Your crocodile tears get our Men murdered
I charge thee
With your failure to come to terms with your own demons

The wickedness you spit into the atmosphere
Has crash landed on your seeds and spawned vines that threaten to
  rise up
And choke us
Forever placing us on our guard
The American dream has given us PTSD
And your haughtiness will be the ruination of civilization

With One Look
Veronica Lac

I saw how you tried to hide the look
of disgust on your face
I saw the glimmer of shame that shook
your image of yourself
you, most liberal, well-meaning of folks
who thinks you're above it all,
the one who knows all the right words
to say, but still the one who falls

That look told me all I needed
to know, that underneath
the gestures of being on my page
hides what's deeply ingrained
to the core of your being
the inherited bias of your race
embodied supremacy and hate
that will never be washed away

From behind your mask, you tried in vain
to hide the fact you moved
away, pulling yourself
to a safer distance, away from
me, this Asian woman's face
just in case, just in case, just in case
I might carry disease
Though it's more likely just your dis-ease

No need for words, no apologies
I see how you see me
But of course, you're not racist, I see
It's just that you're afraid of me
Of what I might carry
Despite my being in the same boat
and that you might just as likely
be the one who has the disease

'Twas Some Weeks Before Christmas (2016)[1]
Nathaniel Granger, Jr.

'Twas some weeks before Christmas, when all thro' the States,
Not a creature was stirring, not even Bill Gates;
The votes were all cast and counted with care,
In hopes that our president would win fair and square;
The people were sleeping all snug in their beds,
While visions of utopia danced in their heads;
The Mrs. in her mumu, my head on her lap,
Had just called it a night for a long winter's nap;
When all of sudden, the silence was shattered,
I sprang from the bed to see what was the matter;
Away to the TV I flew like a flash,
Turned up the volume, and pulled out my stash;
The numbers were rising, as each vote was tallied,
While out in the streets folk started to rally;
When, what to my ears would come like a thump,
The anchor announced we'd elected Donald Trump!
I knew in that moment I was losing my mind,
More rapid than eagles a changing of times;
Now back to the stash as you may have been spying,
The legalized weed kept me from crying;
Nevertheless, during this holiday rift,
Driving are people for last minute gifts;
As if we've forgotten during this hustle and bustle,
That half of a nation is left hoodwinked and puzzled;
Bamboozled and stunned would old Bill agree,
"Why didn't they elect my wife Hillary?"
Well, one thing's for sure despite all the doubt,
Christmas still comes with a dance and a shout;
Out in the streets the children are playing,
While mamas and papas stay watchful and praying;
His glory still shines through all we may do,
His love yet prevails and transcends red and blue;
For if I say it once I do say it thrice,
The joy of the season is because of the Christ;

---

[1] "Twas Some Weeks Before Christmas" was inspired in part by "Twas the Night Before Christmas.

So, may we reflect on not what is profane;
And remember the reason why Jesus came.

My hope for us all is that our hearts always be light
And Merry Christmas to all, and to all a good night.

Honeymoon in Harrisburg

J. Thomas Brown

Leather soled shoes do the get-ahead-shuffle
Camel hair coats glide over the walk
Tight fitting gloves grip black leather handles
Bright eyes stare down at the cracks

Sally two-skirts is walking through town
Sally wears two skirts, one to her knees and one to her thighs
She's got a crazy set of radish eyes and rag doll hair tangled from the
    wind, and she's howling, yelling in the air:
*I want some answers, I want answers now, if nobody can tell me, we'll go
    to Harrisburg, they have answers there*

Two blocks down's a gas station on the corner
There's a trashcan at the curb where toothless Bob has lunch
Bob lifts the lid, finds a couple lucky fries, shoves them between his
hairy lips, then wipes his lizard hands on a tattered coat. The
attendant steps outside and yells so loud you hear him on the other
    side of town:
You're a man, you're a man, you're a man

Bob pretends he doesn't hear—keeps on munching
Sally walks by: *I want some answers, I want them now. Let's go to
    Harrisburg, they have answers there*
Bob puts back the lid. When spring comes, they're nowhere to be
    found

***

"Honeymoon in Harrisburg" was previously published in *Mooncalf* by J.
Thomas Brown (2020, Fenghuang Publishing). Republished with permission.

Chicago Sonnet #29

D. A. Hosek

Don't go thinking you know me
Y'all too scared to drive my vicinity
I see you roll your windows lock your doors
Thinking we all be drug dealers pimps and whores

Sure we hustle and yeah some of us bang
But the rest of us we just wanna hang
On the corner with our buds score some weed
Drink some beer that be all we need

Then the cops come by and shut us down
Rough us up like we all be clown
Throw us to the ground and cuff us good
Ain't no lawyers help out this neighborhood

Treat me like a crook a thug and that who I be
'Cause round here ain't no choice just destiny

Chocolate Bliss
Duane L. Herrmann

I sip my cocoa,
eat my chocolate;
eclairs
are the bringers of bliss.
Can life get any better
than this?
In Africa, in Mali,
Ivory Coast or elsewhere,
some child,
boy or girl,
of eight or ten,
is enslaved and working
for my bliss,
uncared for
by their captors,
but I have my chocolate,
and soon
the child will likely die.

***

"Chocolate Bliss" was previously published in *Remnants of a Life: Poems* by Duane L. Herrmann (2019, Lighted Lake Press). Republished with permission.

The Auctioneer
Y'Anad Burrell

This poem was written as part of an activity in which participants were asked to write a poem in the voice of someone participating in an auction of people who were enslaved in early United States history.

Here's to another Saturday
It's auction time, and I cannot be late
The only job I've had in my life
Handed down to me from my Dad
I preferred to get an education
But I had to put food on the table for the kids
Kids I never wanted but was told it was the right thing to do
...that it was the right path to take
Here's to another empty-soul Saturday

The Auctioneer's Unconscious
Louis Hoffman

This poem was inspired by the poem "Bid 'em In" by Oscar Brown, Jr., performed by Nathaniel Granger, Jr, which tells the story of African slaves being sold on the auction block. This was written as a part of an exercise in which participants were asked to write a response poem to "Bid 'em In" from the perspective of one of the characters in the poem. It was written in the voice of the auctioneer.

I can't let you *in*
I can't
My son is outside
and he needs new shoes
I can't let you in

When I was a child
I saw more deeply
...felt more deeply
the pain
I could sense the injustice
and my bones cried out to speak
But Daddy told me different
And Daddy was a good man
He went to church
Helped our neighbors
when their barn burned down
And he cared for those who were sick
He's a good man
So I...
I can't let you in

You are too powerful
You could shatter my whole world
Take my comforts, my security
My dreams, and even myself
You see, like my Daddy
I am a good man
I love my wife, my children
I help my neighbors
I give to the poor
I am a good man

I *must* be
a good man
And...
I want to stay
a good man
so I can't...
can't let you penetrate
the walls of my heart
I can't let you in

Skating with Our Daughter on Veteran's Day
Carol Barrett

He was born from soil beneath this ice,
clay red with tears, the names of tribes
calling now as I watch his broken back:
Winnebago, Hopi, Sioux. Witness:
we broke his back in Nam,
where the boys skated on mud.
He could not keep them
from falling. He pinned tags
on their stiff toes,
and sent them home.

At least the bones went back.
We broke his back in Nam,
and before that—we broke it.
I watch his stooped ghost
travel this ice, racing
his brothers across their backyard
river, his grandfather's black hair
trailing the Mississippi.

I am here to witness. At least the bones
went back. Not always so:
Cherokee, Chickasaw, Choctaw.
Bones shipped in small
white parcels to stone museums.
Artifacts, we call them:
leather, flint, bone. The severed hands
of his fathers now in Paris,
feet in Munich, ribs scattered
to Rio de Janeiro and Rome.

They are calling in the bones:
Chinook, Cheyenne, Santee,
assembling the teeth,
the wrists of his people,
returning the dead beneath the ice,
raising them high above the snow

in the rattled air of ravens
so souls can rest, his grandfather,
his mother, all the mothers.

Smoke rises:
Makah, Iroquois, Shawnee.
New fires by the ice. Old bones.
In the capital city
the Nations weep, calling
for clavicle, hip bone, skull.
Bones in the Smithsonian
still haunt their graves.
Federal skeletons, exempt
from law: *Pawnee, Delaware, Osage.*
There is no release.

My daughter's small bones on skates
make tiny drums on the ice:
Yakima, Penobscot, Creek.
Her father glides toward me,
back rising, long hair
clinging to his face, lifts her
into the net of my bones.

***

"Skating with Our Daughter on Veteran's Day" was previously published in *Calling in the Bones* by Carol Barrett (Ashland Poetry Press, 2005). Republished with permission from Ashland Poetry Press.

"Skating with Our Daughter on Veteran's Day" was previously published in *Whirlwind Magazine* (May 15, 2015, Issue #4). Republished with permission from the author.

"Skating with Our Daughter on Veteran's Day" was previously published in *Lullabies & Confessions: Poetic Explorations of Parenting Across the Lifespan* edited by Louis Hoffman and Lisa Xochitl Vallejos (University Professors Press, 2021). Republished with permission from University Professors Press.

A Resurrected Woman
Venita R. Thomas

I'm not proclaiming supernatural deity
I'm not proclaiming perfection
I'm not proclaiming entitled selfishness
I'm not proclaiming charitable constipation
I'm proclaiming living beyond survival
I'm proclaiming authenticity, truth and destiny
I'm proclaiming gratitude, not indigenous servitude
I'm proclaiming independence from addiction of approval, shame and
  poverty
I'm proclaiming life, love, green pastures and still waters, peace and
  wealth
I'm proclaiming taking care of myself; I'm proclaiming me.

Church Bells of Moxico
Esther Muthoni Wafula

For how long
Have your loud dongs
Been rousing reluctant children
From their dreams?

For how long
Have your wordless cries
Been sounding fathers' hopes
That lost children will one day be found?

For how long
Have your solemn gongs
Been lending public voice
To mothers' private grief?

For how long
Have your familiar summons
Been calling
Your country's people to prayer?

Do they do your bidding
Or do they think
You are only breaking
The spell of a night's passing?

Note: Moxico is the largest province in Angola. I wrote the poem during my time in Angola, when the civil war there was still raging.

Mass Puddles

Joseph Ellison Brockway

The obfuscated truth of the media
a veil of darkness
the black veil of mothers
grieving their children
reduced to black letters on cold stones
black clouds looming
over a nation in mourning
the veil of mass media
of mass hatred
covering mass shootings
mass projectile excuses
mass constitutional extermination
from the public's gaze
from a veil of mass yellow tape that
segregates and edits out
mass puddles in the streets
where beauty in all its blackness
once shone brighter than any false
gold star of protection
grieve no more, mothers,
put down your funerary fans
a black flicker remains
its incendiary rise will burn
the veil of darkness
no more

Wind's Lyrics of Equality
Kristen Beau Howard

Listen,
the grass in the wind is bending toward a soft wisp of nothing,
     of everything,
     of you.
Chiming of sweet smells from Earth,
in lemon zest and wet dirt,
and the heat of sun which gave birth to its tall and fragile length.
Those keen whispers of grass will stop at once,
into the drifts of winter's white
and into the strangers of night's tail.

Each season—all that is and ever was—delivers this:
the rain fallen drips of swollen griefs, (you know yours by heart)
changing dirt into mud, is swallowed deep down inside Earth's walls
     of lava,
     of molded percolation.
In forgotten distance of upward blanket blue,
the vast sky in holding anew.

Close your eyes.
Listen,
do you hear a blade of grass, of many or few, and in different rhythms?
It was created by rain and mud and sun.

Keep heart these truths:
Your underarms of molten lava will scold a rock,
creating lands of someone's future swollen memories.
For mercy's sake your life is passing.
You do not have to hold your breath
     of sorrows,
     of unmet tomorrows.
But drop your sharp swords of cruel words
that bleed your soul and others.
In open winds the lyrics breathe their own song in flight,
listen.

Snakes in the Trees

J. Thomas Brown

The horsemen are riding
Snakes hang in the trees
The boughs are breaking
As they bend in the wind
The sky's flashing lightning
There's ozone in the air
Get back from the windows
It's safer there

Ma is crying
Her tears rain down
The nephilim are walking
On her holy ground
The earth's pores are bleeding
From the living clay
Goliath is drinking
Its lifeblood away

There're earthquakes in New Madrid
And Azle near Fort Worth
Chimneys are crumbling
Bricks fall to the floor
There's fire in the water
There're snakes in the trees
The tree boughs are breaking
As they bend in the wind

Cattle are dying
The wells have gone bad
The highway is cracking
From down below
The giants are coming
From over the hill
Their hunger is growing
And cannot be quelled

The land has been taken
Without legal grounds
Pipelines encroach
The edge of our towns
Money can't bring back
What they've stolen away
By Halliburton Loopholes
And eminent domain

***

"Snakes in the Trees" was previously published in *Mooncalf* by J. Thomas Brown (2020, Fenghuang Publishing). Republished with permission.

Leaving the Planet
Rachel Porias

My mother died from a digestive disorder
While Alzheimer's stole her memory
And her life
She had experienced a trauma
In her young life
Of which she never spoke
Never wanting to acknowledge her pain
She glided through life
Helping others
My mother was a little rebellious
She always forged an alliance with the underdog
And treated everyone with kindness
Especially those who couldn't speak for themselves
I think she would have been a Buddhist
If she had been informed
The principles by which she lived
But never voiced, came naturally
As a child, I always wondered why the day after a visit to school
My mother would pack a box of clothes
For me to take
"I can still hear my mother's voice:"
"Remember to take the box of clothes to school
"Barbara should have the dresses and bows"
"And the shoes too"
"For James, the brown pants and striped shirts,"
"Socks and shoes"
"Nathan needs the socks, shirts, and underwear,"
"And for Nathan,
"The coat of bright green"
"He is much too lean"

Years later,
On my second day at a residential group home for boys where I
worked,
I carried in a box of clothes,
and I could just hear my mother's voice...
"The shirts and shoes are for Chris,

The khaki pants for Trumaine, and the shoes too,
Don't forget that Malcolm needs underwear and shirts
And a thick coat for the little boy who looks like he is so cold...Burt
As she left the planet
She didn't recognize me anymore
But, one time,
When she was in the hospital,
And I got up
From her bedside to walk across the room
She looked up at me
And cried

Poisoning the Water
Kelsey Smith

There's a wildfire ripping through the sky
And our water protectors are standing through the night
Even though there's nothing fair about this fight
And dawn's early light is still out of sight
But it'll break that horizon, a beacon burning bright
But the rubber bullets already took flight
And the police are rabid dogs ready to bite
Violent escalation has reached a new height
Protect them from the white man
Such a typical plight
And our concerns are dismissed with "oh, it'll be alright"
If I hear it again I will scream
Cause you're just as complacent as you seem
We won't be dictated
By what you deem important
Because your priorities
Are exorbitantly disproportionate
And we won't deal with any more of your extortion
You can rape and impregnate
But we will have our abortion
And as our tears fall softly on the dirt
These sprinkled seeds will erupt in rebirth
A phoenix will rise from the ashes of the earth
But we have to light the fire first

You Can't Commodify the Sacred:
For the Next Seven Generations, of the Colonizer
Gina Belton

I am a water
Protector, BEing prayer
Mni Wiconi

Not a terrorist.
Your projections have no place
In my ceremony

And ... I hold you close
This prayer and ceremony
Also protects you.

Pledge of Allegiance, February 2017
Marna Broekhoff

I pledge allegiance to the flag

Or allegiance to Russia by Trump and Flynn
That is sure to get a financial win
For them. Build that wall into thin air
Hang up on Australia, exit NATO, no loyalty there

To make American great again
We must make America hate again

Of the United States of America

Or blue states, red states, Citizens Disunited
You can talk to your legislator only if invited

To make America great again
We must make America hate again

And to the Republic for which it stands

Unless you have a pre-existing condition
Or somehow need extraordinary rendition

To make America great again
We must make America hate again

One nation under God

With the caveat that where you're from or how you pray
Will surely determine if you come or stay

To make America great again
We must make America hate again

Indivisible

Visible—invisible—are now "alternative facts"
And no one cares for scientific stats

To make America great again
We must make America hate again

With liberty and justice for -- sale!

Human Love
Tracy Lee Sisk

Human love, the kind without a tether.
The kind that bonds, no matter the weather.
Love to be as we are, shaded or bright.
Glue that binds our souls through all of life's plight.
Love that sees into the character's hint.
Pays no attention to the color's tint.
Love that knows differences don't matter.
Solid love doesn't easily shatter.
Eyes that choose to see the common places.
Images etched, no separate races.
Human love, the kind without a tether...
Oh my, wouldn't the world feel a whole lot better?

The Big Burn

Jennifer Lagier

She is a housing advocate
trying to fit single mothers
and more kids than allowed
by the rules
into decent apartments.
Places where deposits
can be paid in installments
and the landlord
doesn't expect sex on demand
as a portion of rent.
Her clients, a family of five,
live in wet caves
carved from riverbank mud.
Later, at the labor camp,
a contractor collects once a week
but never pays Pacific Gas & Electric,
so they do without power.
They relocate to a barn
with blankets on lettuce crates,
no running water.
An eight-year-old boy
reads to his little sister
in a cow stall with candles.
At the inquest, survivors tell
of finding melted baby-doll limbs
among blackened bones,
charred commas of children
transformed to ashes.

A Bright White Light
Frederick K. Foote, Jr.

Brexit wins
Markets roil

Trump rolls with the wind
and fans the flames of
righteous change to
to make America a
great bonfire of
resentments and spite

The UK and the USA
marching backward
to the promised land
of lurid dreams
of a master race
a woman's place
an Eden restored
a plantation renewed
a nightmare's birth

in the lands of
white hands
and pale visions

***

"A Bright White Light" was previously published by *Immix,* May 25, 2017.

Arvena
Katherine Edgren

Jailed for her mental illness:
profound, un-regulate-able.

They couldn't decide what to do with her
ranting on the streets.

When she couldn't breathe
she begged for her medicine

but they refused to listen
to the ravings of a lunatic—

saw no need to check her fat chart to see
if her condition warranted medicine.

This time they were wrong
and she was,

unfortunately,
correct.

She was in cardiac arrest when they found her,
face blue, airway clenched,

and no amount of wishing could revive a mind
stirred to composing cartoons,
dance steps, songs.

After she was gone, her family sued.

It wasn't the jail's guilt the lawyers disagreed about,
but the monetary value to place on a life so full of temper.

Because I Could Not Stop for Hate[2]
Susan White

For Tamir Rice and the nine victims of Morris Brown A.M.E. Church

Because I could not stop for Death —
The racist stopped for me —
The Cop Car held the right to Kill—
And Blind Brutality.

I slowly turned—to face the man
And I had put away
My toy gun and my childhood, too,
But, he Moved Hastily.

He passed the Point of no Return
In Blood he Stepped too far—
He passed the Truth and Golden Rule
He passed his Golden Star—

Or rather —It passed Us —
The Lead ripped through my Abdomen—
For only Human was my Flesh—
My Color—only Skin—

We passed an Alabama Church
Burnt Rubble on the Ground
The Hate-blocked Selma bridge
The Memphis shot heard 'round.

Since slavery—'Tis a century—and yet
Just the other Day
A white boy with a Loaded Gun
Blew nine, black souls Away—

***

---

[2] "Because I Could Not Stop for Hate" was inspired by "Because I Could Not Stop for Death" by Emily Dickinson.

"Because I Could Not Stop for Hate" was previously published in *Measure Review*. Republished with permission.

When We Let Live
Larry Graber

It starts when
people do not
say "men are X"

When people
hold a space
to reach
beyond and
through
each
and
every
stereotype

We Stand

In front
and among

Face to face

full
and
beautiful

unique
and
strong

Not holding
back
because
of the
Role
we think
we must
play

must
put on
or strip
from another

Full embrace
and stand

see,
believe
hold

we give birth

it starts
when
we can
let be
and
live

Choked-Off Scream
Katherine Rosemond

I see you
Emergency Responder
Warrior
Running into danger
Fighting flames
Protecting life
Ever on guard
Always on duty

We fought
Relentless battles
Saved many lives
Yet tragedy
Often won
Blood
Death
Shook our hearts
Wounded our souls

The calling
So young
To be a savior
A hero

Heroes are tough
Heroes don't weep

Dress uniforms
We stand
In formation lines
Silent statues
With
Invisible eyes
Jaws
Set hard
Against
Swallowed anguish

Burning inside
Saluting
Our countless fallen
Sounds of
pipe and drum
Wails of the bereaved

Our humanity
Denied
Shamed
Locked in the vault
Deep
In our bowels
Screaming
To indifferent
Cold
Unyielding
Walls of stone

A life
Of choked-off cries
Suffocated tears

No medicine
For the bleeding
Agony
Hidden beneath
Thick armor

Haunted

No rest
No peace

Comfort
Is a river
Of whiskey
And wine

I see you,
Brothers

Sisters

My arms
Are open
Hands outstretched
Come
Feel my embrace
Exhale
Let go
Your scream
Won't break you
Let the facade fall away
Fortress walls crumble
Shake
With the trembling earth
Subsiding
Into
Sacred Stillness

A lost reunion

New grass
Warm mud
Wet
With morning dew
Await our feet

Sun
Moon
Ancient stars
Bless the ground
The unfolding journey
Before us

Take my hand
Walk with me

Battle Cry
Sarah Dickenson Snyder

Does it always come back to the rib,
the way we were made in myth—
what stories we live with.

Let's refinance womanhood,
claim our rightful place in the avalanche
of everything-man.

Womb, not wo-man. Let's make
new words, dig through the jewels
in a pyramid for the gems of us.

We are not nothingness. We are
the speed of relief, the ones with milk
in every cell to feed the world.

Servant Leadership
Laura Wright

Oftentimes it gets misrepresented
and even then the truth is still in some
ways circumvented imagine that.

When followers look up to those who
promise to show the way to better days
instead they're left with lies and delays.

Why must it be so hard to do what you
promised without leaving lasting scars
so many innocent fathers still behind bars?

Fenced in by a system that was built against
them and yet you wonder why there are echoes and
cries no justice no peace it's blood in these streets.

How many must perish before the world begins
to cherish the lives lost so carelessly or is that too
much to ask because your privilege gives you a pass.

Wake up and smell the reality your seniority doesn't
justify those fatalities, nor does it stand on any
principalities but you continue to put them in categories.

Just a hypocrite throwing fits until the shoe is on
the other foot and your sons are staring at the barrel
of an officer's gun then what, it's his turn to press
his luck or be shot down like chuck.

Until you stand up for true change then it's best to
remain in your lane and let the ones fighting for
equal rights shine their lights bright as the morning
sun again this is how our freedom began.

It was one man's dream, and another man's legacy yes,
together we shall rewrite history one day and moment

at a time, no longer color blind a strong hand holding mine powerfully combined united in this, Servant Leadership.

from (an elegy, too)
TS Hawkins

I am from the wanton need to just "be"
from my grandfather's last breath at the supremic hands of racism
　　　　my nana's grasp for the future
　　　　　　　my mother's pluck for life
other strong femmes who concede their power to weakened
patriarchal beliefs
　　　　　　shattered homes,
　　　　　scaffolded hope,
and desired structure
from a lexicon of emotional illiteracy
I am from a Baptist, a Catholic, and a soul baptized in the blood of
　　erasure
where love is speculative fiction and heartbreak historically self-help

I am from the wanton need to discover
from an understanding that family isn't a monolith;
　　　　　　j o u r n e y i n g free **and fixed**; yet
I am from the midnight train to Georgia
the Black southern barbeques unioned against northern ideation
　　　　spices old,
　　　　new,
　　　　and unseen
I am from suburban aspirations private schooled in public gardens
and jerseyed in the desperate need to breathe

I am from the wanton need to feel
from epigenetic dreams that salve the temporal monotony
　　　　　　the nightmares,
　　　　　　joy,
　　　　　　and lust for the unfamiliar
I am from the me I see when no one is watching
from homeland stolen to profit oppression
from unsuited expectations
from the me unraveled
from broken traditions; mores lessened for sanity
I am from obligations and fear
　　　　　　　　and rubber,

and glue,
and elastic edges
and
I am from the sharp end of the spear
from Oya —
the protective goddess to Gullah the islands of my legacy, and
I am from the wanton need
to stand despite
to yonder past plank politics
to handsome and beauty unencumbered
to just "be"

Pavement
John C. Mannone

Black leather shoes slap the pavement,
scrape their soles on gravel drive, slip
on Kentucky grass—officer in pursuit
of the perp, a two-eleven in progress.

There's always an elegance to flying
tackles, swift movements to shackle
the thief, while adrenaline courses
through the veins of pavement-hard
hearts.

The pavement to the courthouse
has been well-worn by the shuffle
of lawyerly papers lining courtrooms
along halls of justice paved with good
intentions—so is the road to hell.

Plain concrete—cement, aggregate,
water in a 1:2:4 mixture—is not high
in tensile strength but still will not
buckle & yield to the force

of a knee on the neck, a criminal
body spread prostrate on pavement
is still innocent until proven guilty.

No Rite of Passage
Shelley Lynn Pizzuto

We have been standing here bending in the wind
Shining sun through the eyes in support of your way finding
You have been calling us for lifetimes now
Blind and calling
We had shed the dress and into the pants
Slipping back now into the dress
Shoulders are relaxed, chests bare and open
Our bellies slightly distended as we can no longer erode the push
To birth
Our minds
Our voice
Our restoration
We have walked silently at your side for centuries now
Adorned with jewels and burned at stakes
Keeping us untouchable and charred
We are not of the shame you fear for desiring our breast
No envy for the phallus held between the legs
We only wish to see you rise
Out of the ground and down from the top of the world
Meeting us here in the middle
Taking a spot beside us

Asking for Names
Nance Reynolds

Here I stand at dusk.
Listening
  to the rhythm of the winds.
Even with this golden pink light
  as it partners with mountain, hillock and grove...
Mostly, I listen.
Over and over I hear these words,
I can't breathe. Never Again.

Winds ebb and flow, long grasses rustle in reply
  as they brush my ankles and knees with their sharp edges.
Silhouettes are painted with stark lines
  as night approaches tenderly.
I imagine the wind is speaking through centuries.

A chime is rung from afar.
Asking
  for the names of all cherished.
Each name is weighted and hanging in mountain air.
Each name is a clear and precious drop of rain,
Here, in the center of my pounding, aching heart.

Echoing through valley walls our cries resound,
  of inhumanity lived and witnessed each day.
Cries piercing heart and breath,
    rock, air, and time,
and still, the slow golden-edged shadows roll across the land.

We offer water to one another in cupped hands,
as we gather on ancient and crumbling steps.
One said to another, is this our chosen way?

Untitled Black Man
Kelsey Smith

If you made it through today
Without feeling any rage
I condemn you
In a system that preys on blackness
We're all victims until we tackle this
I won't defend you.
Have the guts to stand up to the corrupt
Don't let them speak,
Silence them
Interrupt.
Will this end soon?
Murdered in the streets by our protectors
Futures coming and we're the electors
It's opportune
The water's churning, a whirlpool's forming
Clouds move in and soon it'll be storming
Bring the monsoon
We're all ants being crushed under your feet
But we'll all gather and soon our eyes will meet
Once in a blue moon.
I hope you feel the fear you've spread
Martyrs are breaking their last bread
And they're coming for you.

Threatened by Beads
Red Haircrow

When they see beads they ask, 'How much?'
because they assume you're selling and for sale.
But beads outside their ken,
their 'showcase-our-pet-native' events,
their museums holding us hostage in basement boxes,
Unsettle, alarm, concern them as old fears return.
Hand-me-down tales of witless savagery and
indigenous aggression, indigenous spat like a curse.

All the while conveniently forgetting
their invasion and abuses demanded native attention,
and that however curious their faces now,
they resemble those who raped and killed us.
The ones who lamented and prayed
for our poor lost savage souls while
calling our passing inevitable and our
genocide 'survival of the fittest'.

Now with mobile phones and synthetic fiber clothes,
they wear fake headdresses at weekend festivals,
or claim to be our sacred prophecies fulfilled.
They insist they're honoring us and preserving
our cultures while bidding over our bones and
defending mascots making our children bleed.

Killing by appropriation is the thing these days,
but wearing beads without permission is a crime,
and braided hair for tradition is militant
from the viewpoint of the oppressor and oppressed.
But some keep tossing back their whiskey words,
saying, 'It's alright, let them dance,'
finding humor in theft.

Some of us won't smile with you,
won't lie with you and even our wordless presence
makes you uncomfortable then angry:
for your anger comes from fear.

Fear that we just might justifiably
call in debts from the centuries old bloody account
from which you keep making withdrawals.

***

"Threatened by Beads" was previously published in *Red Ink International Journal,* December 2016. Republished with permission.

"Threatened by Beads" was previously published in *Geschichte Schrieben- Neue Rundschau*, 2018. Republished with permission.

A Matter of Conscience
Jennifer Lagier

for Maria Corralejo

First I see the
women cannery workers on strike
whose only bargaining tools
consist of eight days
of prayer and self-imposed hunger.

Today, Sureño gang members
carry management-provided weapons,
patrol concertina wire corridors
between busloads of scabs
and picket-line labor.

My friend,
the tenth child
of immigrant field hands,
describes 400 women and children
falling to their knees,
dragging themselves slowly
in protest
toward a church
down the Watsonville highway.

Sometimes, she tells me,
there is nothing left
to place between greed
and the poor
except our own bodies.

***

"A Matter of Conscience" was previously published in *Solidarity, 37*(9), September 1994. Republished with permission.

Michael Brown, Jr: A Postscript
Bernardine (Dine) Watson

After the flash
the shock
the fury
a vast and beautiful darkness
a wing-ed silence
that has fluttered now and then
at the corner of my eye
then flown away
leaving me
to bear the bitter jangle of my lot.

Feel my pain
Feel my pain
My own mother don't give a damn
I got money on my mind
And I ain't got the time
Tryin' a nickel and a dime
Just to make a rhyme.

I always was a sensitive boy
Big Mike: stone trap rapper
straight out of Ferguson
writing lyrics on scraps of paper
the way they came into my head
and storing them in a jar
at my grandma's house
don't move me, don't move me
let me lie here where I fell
on the cold hard ground
let the sun burn my flesh
let the birds drink my blood
 this is where I'm from.

When the sun goes down
On my side of town
Well you in trouble now
Devil get up off my back

Break it down bag it up
Feel my pain
Feel my pain.

How peaceful to be
as big as the sky
but who knew such peace
could only come to me this way?
a walk down the street
a pack of cigarillos
I took to calm my nerves
I heard that god don't make mistakes
one day the whole world
is going to know my name.

Feel my pain
Feel my pain.

Angry. Black. Woman.
Jennifer O'Neill

Yes, I'm Angry, Yes, I'm Black, Yes, I'm a woman
Does that make me an Angry Black Woman?
They told me I have a lump in my breast
Too small to do anything about

Two months later,
The lump demands to be seen by the naked eye
It speaks up like the unnoticed child
Suddenly it's emergent.
I must voluntarily submit myself to the knife.
Deconstructed and dismembered
Something must be taken from me
Again

I lived through it like I've lived through everything else
being a brave solider
In the war against me, the war against my body
my existence
If that wasn't enough,
I was snatched from my bedroom
my recovery room, safe room.
Forced to leave my home, pulled out of my temporary comfort
To buy pandemic toilet paper

No time to grieve
Yet again
no stillness
yet again
no reprieve
yet again
no recovery
again
I don't want to be strong damn it
I don't want to suck it up
I want to stay in bed and be held
I want to be swaddled and nurtured
By my mother

By my sisters
By my lover
No! I don't get that privilege

I must go from store to store
In the coldness of the world before the sun shows its face
Searching
Again
For what I need
What I must provide

Yes, I'm a Black woman holding her bandaged breast
Searching with my 80-year-old mother next to me.
She's searched before
For damn toilet paper
And again, I find
None left for me

I Pray You Pardon Me
Jennifer K. Yancey

Please, Sir, can you refrain from putting
Your laws on my body?
Your patriarchy is most uncomfortable
About 400 years too small
Definitely not a fit for my femme mystique ~
Oh is my self-possession too loud for you?
I pray you pardon me.

No you cannot will me to my knees
Force my head down as if bobbing for apples
Only to come up with assorted nuts
Too inadequate, so you rather I not be heard and
Barely even seen
But you can't dim my shine, clown
So step aside and pardon me.

B---h,
Put that phone down
Your sensitivity makes you lose all your poise
Calling the cops with all that "white noise"
Just accept your inferiority
Eff off and leave me be!
Every lie you spin becomes the death of We
And, even then, they still won't pardon me.

Father, forgive me
For I *know* what I do
Conscious of my conscience
That wants to give way to my rising flesh
Cause ruckus,
Lose my religion,
And my finesse
Help me quell the beast
My thoughts alone qualify as
Unbearable sin
Give me wisdom of when to speak
Ears to hear and eyes to see
And if I slip and fall from grace

In Jesus' name ~
I pray You pardon me.

Reflection
Nancy Devine

He's leaning as deep into the mirror
as he can in the morning
in the boys' restroom
at the school where I teach.

Not sequestered by the urinals,
the sinks, the stalls...
in plain view at the open entrance
where he lines his eyes
usually his right,
right hand pulling his eye taut
left following
the eye's curve below the lower lashes
where smudged charcoal color looks
especially tough and androgynous
David Bowie and Patty Smith and Robert Smith

I and whoever passes
are supposed to see this primping,
the broad strokes of it,
implication and meaning,
concealment and revelation.
Why else in such plain sight?

Now what direction? For him,
east would be out.
Not back into the womb
where boys are first girls
then the body cannot be bent
into what it never really was.
What his mother or father
or guardian is protected from
unless they would walk the halls with me
before the bell rings.
I don't even know his name.

Revised Second Amendment
Frederick K. Foote, Jr.

A well-regulated Militia
of mass murders
being necessary to
the [in]security
of a [un]free State
held hostage to the
deprivations of the
AR-15-style assault rifle
the right of the people
to keep and bear arms
and the burden of blood
carnage and growing rage
shall not be infringed.

***

"Revised Second Amendment" was previously published in *The Progressive Standard*, July 4, 2016

Vashti Reviews Linda Lovelace
Carol Barrett

It is my story too:
the queen smiles, they won't believe
the flowered bruises
under lights, gun to her head.
It could have been
an inlaid silver knife
waiting in its velvet sheath.

Men in silk ties
rip her insides, five at once.
The next scene threatens
a dog, a donkey.
It could have been
a camel's tongue, a goat's horn.

Rape is rape.
Always, someone ready
to snatch the glove
of evil, play god,
dismember a life, film
the killing, sell it.

You endure what you can.
For the rest, there is
a numbing of parts
and a plotting, somewhere deep,
deeper than the flowered passage
to the womb, the rectum,
deeper than the throat
with its copper taste
of strangulation, deeper
than blood, unreachable
deep, the hidden
cloister, all of us
violate and alive.

Congratulations. Another queen
refuses her captor.
Out of the king's lair. Out
of bondage. Go quickly.
The rape is still playing.

***

"Vashti Reviews Linda Lovelace" was previously published in *The Unauthorized Book of Esther: New Poems and Commentary on Revisionist Biblical Literature* by Carol Barrett (1998; Doctoral Dissertation, Union Institute and University, Cincinnati, OH). Reprinted with permission from the author.

"Vashti Reviews Linda Lovelace" was previously published in *Steam Ticket* (Spring, 2017, 20, 19-20). Reprinted with permission.

All Are Welcome
Melinda Rose

Well, sure all are welcome
It's a church meeting after all.
Well, sure all are welcome
We want enough good folks to fill this hall.
Well, sure all are welcome
From the temple, the tabernacle, the mosque
Oh...from the mosque?
Nope, don't you come—not at all.

Call for the Question
Nathaniel Granger, Jr.

Crumbling neighborhoods
No neighbors, just hoods
But not the white hoods
Only the ones making Trayvon look suspicious
Rendering him guilty
Rendering him dead
From the grave crying justice
From the grave seeing just us
Call for the question

Failing economy, homeless souls
Poor schools,
Abandoned housing tell stories of crack
Lack of services along this route
From the uber the signs speak of glam:
Michigan, Lombard, Rodeo, and Broadway
From the street, the signs scream, "Damn!"
"Please help, need food, God Bless," anyway...
Call for the question

Battering, rape, child abuse
Interpersonal violence at an all-time high
Like 4:20 high
But without laugh, without the buzz, without chill
Except the chill that runs down the degenerative spine
Of the chronically oppressed
Perplexed, distressed, microaggressed
Leaving its victim depressed and helpless
Call for the question

Allow me to quote
The 25th letter of the alphabet
"Y"
Y do Black Lives Matter
Only in theory, only it's scary
Y do we think racism is a phase
From forgotten days

When the fear today
Is the threat of death
And at a minimum, TAZED

Y do the rich get richer
The poor get poorer
The religious leaders
Serve the gods of their bellies
Forgetting the hungry, hopeless sinner
Y do the politicians
Talk of walls and deportation
Instead of harmony and integration
It's high time that we as a nation
Call for the question

One move for gender neutral
Another, segregation
Marijuana recreation
Gun control, drug control
Panhandling control
Control-top pantyhose
And yet, we're out of control
Moving faster and faster forward
And getting nowhere
In a hurry to get nowhere fast
Before we carry another motion
Call for the question.

We Shall Not Go Back!
Hubert C. Jackson, Jr.

The last time that the United States Capitol was breached
by a hostile element it was a foreign force,
the British army unleashing its effort to subdue
the infant, rebel government
of a group of upstart colonies thrusting for freedom.
The Capitol was burned, democracy was threatened,
and our Colonial leaders were forced to flee.
A war was fought, by both slave and free,
and together, although facing
tremendous disadvantages,
with the assistance of foreign allies,
they committed their all
to the fight.
Although sometimes ragged and tattered,
tired, hungry, some with
frost-bitten feet,
they vanquished that invading foe
causing them a hasty retreat
to their ships that they might take flight.
We shall not go back!

On January 6, 2021,
Two-hundred and seven years,
after the British
sacked and burned
the White House and US Capitol,
the United States Capitol
was once again breached by a hostile element,
this time,
citizens of the United States of America,
incited to insurrection
by a sitting United States President,
had as their mission to overturn
the confirmation of a legitimate election,
the voice of the people,
 by force.
Once again this shrine of democracy

suffered physical damage,
and lives were needlessly lost.
The efforts of those
who would have denied the validation
of this democratic action
also failed and freedom continues to reign.
We shall not go back!

We shall not go back
by threat of intimidation from any element or force,
either foreign or domestic.
The covers have been pulled back
and the true threat to democracy for all has been revealed.
The ugliness of racial hatred
 that festered below the surface
was given presidential permission
to run amuck for four years and culminated
in a crisis on Capito Hill
and the world witnessed
the poster child of democracy stumble.
But we shall regain our footing
and maintain our nation's course
to securing that more perfect, all-inclusive union,
relegating none to subservience
while affording each an opportunity to advance
and achieve
while making a positive contribution
to keeping our country on that course.
We shall not kowtow to that
misguided, hate-filled, prejudice-oriented
element that would keep us divided
as a people.
We will not go back!

Activities

The activities in this section are intended to facilitate your social justice involvement as well as show how reading, writing, and performing poetry can be a part of this work. Some activities focus more generally on social justice work while others focus more specifically on poetry. The intention is to use these activities to inform your writing and your social justice engagement.

Activity 1: Social Justice Priorities
Make a list of the social justice issues that you are committed to. This can be done over a week or more to make sure that it is inclusive. After the list is complete, spend some time reflecting and journaling on your level of commitment to and your level of knowledge about each issue. As you do this, it can help to do some research. Also, you may read and write poems relevant to these social justice issues to help deepen your thoughts and emotional connection to each issue. Try to organize your list in terms of your priorities, your knowledge, and which issues you believe you can most effectively make a solid commitment to. After this, let your list rest for a week. As you return to the list, begin considering how this can inform your future social justice work.

Activity 2: What Would Social Justice Look Like?
Identify a particular social justice issue that you are passionate about. Spend some time reflecting on what social justice would look like for this issue. Then write a poem about your reflection on what social justice would look like for this issue.

Activity 3: Self-Care
Spend some time reflecting or journaling about your self-care needs relevant to social justice work and how you can get those needs met. If you find yourself stuck on how to meet these needs, it may be beneficial to discuss this with a friend, colleague, or possibly a therapist. As you clarify your needs, consider writing a poem about this.

Activity 4: Social Justice Exemplars and Mentors
Identify a social justice exemplar or mentor. If you do not have sufficient information about this individual, spend some time reading up on them.

Next, write a poem about them or a poem in their voice. After you have finished the poem, spend some time reflecting or journaling about what you can learn from them for your own social justice work.

Activity 5: Bid 'Em In
Listen to Oscar Brown's recording of "Bid 'Em In" on YouTube (https://www.youtube.com/watch?v=UgRexzlTn9g). After listening to the reading of the poem, write a poem in the voice of a character that you imagine as part of the scene. You may also consider trying this with the following Rhiannon Giddens songs or poem by Nathaniel Granger, Jr.:

- Song: "Julie" by Rhiannon Giddens
  (https://www.youtube.com/watch?v=zu5ZYXi6EiE)
- Song: "At the Purchaser's Option" by Rhiannon Giddens
  (https://www.youtube.com/watch?v=6vy9xTS0QxM)
- Poem: "'Dat 'Der Book" by Nathaniel Granger, Jr.
  (https://youtu.be/o41fXAXRqxE)

Activity 6: Response Poems
Choose one of the poems in this volume that has impacted you. Spend some time reading and reflecting upon the poem. After you have done this, write your own response poem. Set these aside a few days or a week. Then return to the original poem and your response poem and read them together.

Activity 7: Daily Awareness
Commit to keeping a log of the instances of microaggressions, prejudice, and discrimination that you witness for a period of two weeks. You can focus broadly on various forms of experience or focus more discretely on a particular type, such as racism, sexism, or homophobia. After the two weeks, spend some time reviewing these encounters, paying particular attention to the emotions this evokes in you. As you sit with the emotions, allow for a poem to form.

Activity 8: Daily Immersion
Commit to reading a poem from *Rising Voices* each morning for a period of one month. When you read the poem, allow yourself to sit with the emotions and lessons from the poem as you begin your day. During the period of reading poems, keep a journal of your awareness, emotions, and thoughts. You may also find some of your own poems emerging from the reflection and journaling.

Activity 9: Self-Awareness

Sue (2010) defined microaggressions as "Brief and commonplace daily verbal, behavioral, and environmental indignities, whether intentional or unintentional, that communicates hostile, derogatory, or negative racial, gender, sexual orientation, and religion slights and insults to the target person or group" (p. 5).[1] Spend some time reflecting about a circumstance when you engaged in a microaggression. Notice your emotions, your thoughts, the context, and what you learned from this experience. After you have spent some time with this, write a poem. The poem could take different approaches, such as:

1. Write a poem in the voice of the person or one of the person(s)[2] who was impacted by your microaggression. Consider how they may have been impacted by your words or actions.
2. Write a poem in your own voice, reflecting the different aspects of your experience. Part of the power of poetry is that it can hold paradox and divergent experiences together.
3. Write a poem in the voice of the person or one of the person(s) impacted by your microaggression followed by a response poem in your own voice.

Activity 10: Images & Poetry

Find an image that, for you, represents a social justice issue. This can be an image from social media, the internet, or print; or you can use an image from a photo that you have taken. Spend some time with this image reflecting upon the scene. Pay attention to aspects of the poem that stand out, the context that the photo reveals, your emotional reaction to the poem, and your thoughts as you look at the image. After you have spent some time in reflection, write a poem. This poem can describe what is transpiring in the reflections that you experienced as you immersed yourself in the image. Alternatively, the poem could be written from the

---

[1] Sue, D. W. (2010). *Microaggressions in everyday life: Race, gender, sexual orientation.* John Wiley & Sons.

[2] When writing a poem in the voice of another person, especially when it is the voice of someone from a different social position, it is important to be careful and thoughtful when sharing this poem with others. These poems can be useful in developing empathy and a different perspective; however, it is important to recognize that the poems likely do not represent an accurate understanding of the other person and not to assume they reflect accurate empathy. Generally, it is best to keep these poems to oneself for one's own personal use and growth.

perspective of a person or object in the poem (i.e., what would the handcuffs in an image of an encounter between a police officer and a BIPOC individual say?).

Alternate Approach: Keep a camera, which could be a camera in a phone, handy. Take your own photo that represents a social justice issue. Use this image for reflection and writing the poem.

About the Editors

Louis Hoffman, PhD, is the Executive Director of the Rocky Mountain Humanistic Counseling and Psychological Association, and a psychologist in private practice. An avid writer, he has 20 books and over 100 journal articles and book chapters to his credit. He is the 2020/2021 recipient of the Rollo May Award from the Society for Humanistic Psychology. He has been recognized as a Fellow of the American Psychological Association and six of its divisions (1, 10, 32, 36, 48, 52) for his contributions to the field of professional psychology. Dr. Hoffman serves on the editorial board of the *Journal of Humanistic Psychology*, *The Humanistic Psychologist*, the *Journal of Constructivist Psychology*, and *Janus Head*. Dr. Hoffman lives in beautiful Colorado Springs with his wife, three sons, and two dogs. He enjoys bicycle riding on the trails of Colorado, hiking, and spending time with his family.

Nathaniel Granger, Jr., PsyD, is a past president of the Society for Humanistic Psychology (American Psychological Association Division 32) and the recipient of the Hari Camari Early Career Award from the Society for Humanistic Psychology. Dr. Granger is a sought-after speaker with several publications, presentations, workshops, and keynotes to his credit. Additionally, he serves as the Treasurer of the Rocky Mountain Humanistic Counseling and Psychological Association and is the founder and director of Be REAL Ministries, Inc., where he serves the community by working closely with marginalized groups as a pastor and registered psychotherapist. Originally from Chicago, Dr. Granger along with his wife and family, has made Colorado Springs home.

Veronica Lac, PhD, LPC, is a mental health professional who works with horses. She is the Founder & Executive Director of The HERD Institute® which offers training and certification in equine facilitated psychotherapy and learning. She has published two books within the field of equine therapy and multiple peer-reviewed articles on the subject. Dr. Lac has served on the Executive Board of APA Division 32 (Secretary) and is a founding member of the Racial Diversity Work Group for the Professional Association of Therapeutic Horsemanship (PATH Intl). She is also a regular peer-reviewer for *The Humanistic Psychologist* and the *Journal of Humanistic Psychology*. Her commitment to fighting for social justice is woven through the fabric of her professional and personal life. Dr. Lac lives on a farm in Orlando, Florida, with her husband, three horses, three dogs, a cat, and six chickens.

Contributor biographies can be found on the University Professors Press website at https://universityprofessorspress.com/poetry-healing-and-growth-series-contributors/

About the Cover Artist

Shanah Leaf Cooley is a local mural artist in the Colorado Springs and Denver area. She graduated from Palmer High School in 2013 and decided to stay local to pursue her degree and play Division II basketball. After graduating from the University of Colorado Colorado Springs in 2018 with her Bachelor of Arts Degree, she continued working as an artist and began her journey as an art educator. She currently teaches middle school art in District 20. Shanah Cooley has a passion for portraying people in her work, specifically minority women.

The piece "Phases" emphasizes the difficulties that come at us in life, often through circumstances out of our control, and the changes that inevitably overcome us in the process. The shards of glass represent the challenges that we face that can "tint" or change our perception about the world around us. This isn't necessarily a bad thing though if we are committed to learning, understanding, and expanding. The phrase "seeing through rose colored glasses" comes to mind, as we get to choose to see the best through this lens. "Phases" honors the challenges we face that change us as a natural part of life, but we can choose to see the best in even the worst circumstances.

Also Available from University Professors Press

Stay Awhile:
POETIC NARRATIVES
ON MULTICULTURALISM
AND DIVERSITY

by Louis Hoffman
and Nathaniel Granger, Jr.

Other Books by the Editors

Humanistic Approaches to Multiculturalism and Diversity: Perspectives on Existence and Difference
Edited by Louis Hoffman, Heatherlyn Cleare-Hoffman, Nathaniel Granger, Jr., & David St. John

Existential Psychology East-West (Volume 1; Revised & Expanded Edition)
Edited by Louis Hoffman, Mark Yang, Francis J. Kaklauskas, Albert Chan, & Monica Mansilla

Existential Psychology East-West (Volume 2)
Edited by Louis Hoffman, Mark Yang, Monica Mansilla, Jason Dias, Michael Moats, and Trent Claypool

Silent Screams: Poetic Journeys Through Addiction & Recovery
Edited by Nathaniel Granger, Jr., & Louis Hoffman

It's Not About the Activity: Thinking Outside the Toolbox in Equine Facilitated Psychotherapy and Learning
By Veronica Lac

Equine-Facilitated Psychotherapy and Learning: The Human-Equine Relational Development (HERD) Approach
By Veronica Lac